Manhattan Review

Test Prep & Admissions Consulting

Turbocharge Your GRE Analytical Writing Guide

(December 16th, 2011)

- ☐ *Answers to real AWA topics*

- ☐ *Comprehensive strategies for both issue-based and argument-based questions*

- ☐ *Emphasis on* How to ideate

- ☐ *Structured approach to brainstorm essay prompt*

- ☐ *Detailed 4-step process for two 30-minute Analytical Writing tasks*

- ☐ *Four essays with 4 versions (Scored 6/5/3/2) with their critiques*

- ☐ *Tips on improving vocabulary and language*

- ☐ *A comprehensive collection of quotes according to themes*

- ☐ *40 essays with analysis templates*

www.manhattanreview.com

Copyright and Terms of Use

10-Digit International Standard Book Number: (ISBN: 1629260088)
13-Digit International Standard Book Number: (ISBN: 978-1-62926-008-2)

Last updated on December 16, 2011.

Manhattan Review, 275 Madison Avenue, Suite 424, New York, NY 10025.
Phone: +1 (212) 316-2000. E-Mail: info@manhattanreview.com. Web: www.manhattanreview.com

About the Turbocharge your GRE Series

The *Turbocharge your GRE* series is designed to be clear and comprehensive. It is the set of tools you need to build the success you seek. Manhattan Review has created these guides to lead you through the complexities of the examination and achieve your best possible result. As so many students before you have discovered, our books break down the different test sections in a careful, clear manner and zero in on exactly what you need to know to raise your score. The complete series is designed to be your best GRE test prep companion as you navigate the road to a successful outcome.

- ■ **GRE Analytical Writing Guide (ISBN: 978-1-62926-008-2)**
- □ **GRE Vocabulary Builder (ISBN: 978-1-62926-009-9)**

About the Company

Manhattan Review's origin can be traced directly to an Ivy-League MBA classroom in 1999. While lecturing on advanced quantitative subjects to MBAs at Columbia Business School in New York City, Prof. Dr. Joern Meissner was asked by his students to assist their friends, who were frustrated with conventional GMAT preparation options. He started to create original lectures that focused on presenting the GMAT content in a coherent and concise manner rather than a download of voluminous basic knowledge interspersed with so-called "tricks." The new approach immediately proved highly popular with GMAT students, inspiring the birth of Manhattan Review. Over the past 15+ years, Manhattan Review has grown into a multi-national firm, focusing on GMAT, GRE, LSAT, SAT, and TOEFL test prep and tutoring, along with business school, graduate school and college admissions consulting, application advisory and essay editing services.

About the Founder

Professor Joern Meissner, the founder and chairman of Manhattan Review has over twenty-five years of teaching experience in undergraduate and graduate programs at prestigious business schools in the USA, UK and Germany. He created the original lectures, which are constantly updated by the Manhattan Review Team to reflect the evolving nature of the GMAT GRE, LSAT, SAT, and TOEFL test prep and private tutoring. Professor Meissner received his Ph.D. in Management Science from Graduate School of Business at Columbia University (Columbia Business School) in New York City and is a recognized authority in the area of Supply Chain Management (SCM), Dynamic Pricing and Revenue Management. Currently, he holds the position of Full Professor of Supply Chain Management and Pricing Strategy at Kuehne Logistics University in Hamburg, Germany. Professor Meissner is a passionate and enthusiastic teacher. He believes that grasping an idea is only half of the fun; conveying it to others makes it whole. At his previous position at Lancaster University Management School, he taught the MBA Core course in Operations Management and originated three new MBA Electives: Advanced Decision Models, Supply Chain Management, and Revenue Management. He has also lectured at the University of Hamburg, the Leipzig Graduate School of Management (HHL), and the University of Mannheim. Professor Meissner offers a variety of Executive Education courses aimed at business professionals, managers, leaders, and executives who strive for professional and personal growth. He frequently advises companies ranging from Fortune 500 companies to emerging start-ups on various issues related to his research expertise. Please visit his academic homepage www.meiss.com for further information.

Manhattan Review Advantages

▶ **Time Efficiency and Cost Effectiveness**

- The most limiting factor in test preparation for most people is time.
- It takes significantly more teaching experience and techniques to prepare a student in less time.
- Our preparation is tailored for busy professionals. We will teach you what you need to know in the least amount of time.

▶ **High-quality and dedicated instructors who are committed to helping every student reach her/his goals**

▶ **Manhattan Review's team members have combined wisdom of**

- Academic achievements
- MBA teaching experience at prestigious business schools in the US and UK
- Career success

Visit us often at www.ManhattanReview.com.
(Select International Locations for your local content!)

International Phone Numbers & Official Manhattan Review Websites

Manhattan Headquarters	+1-212-316-2000	www.manhattanreview.com
USA & Canada	+1-800-246-4600	www.manhattanreview.com
Australia	+61-3-9001-6618	www.manhattanreview.com
Austria	+1-212-316-2000	www.review.at
Belgium	+32-2-808-5163	www.manhattanreview.be
China	+1-212-316-2000	www.manhattanreview.cn
Czech Republic	+1-212-316-2000	www.review.cz
France	+33-1-8488-4204	www.review.fr
Germany	+49-89-3803-8856	www.review.de
Greece	+1-212-316-2000	www.review.com.gr
Hong Kong	+852-5808-2704	www.review.hk
Hungary	+1-212-316-2000	www.review.co.hu
India	+1-212-316-2000	www.review.in
Indonesia	+1-212-316-2000	www.manhattanreview.com
Ireland	+1-212-316-2000	www.gmat.ie
Italy	+39-06-9338-7617	www.manhattanreview.it
Japan	+81-3-4589-5125	www.manhattanreview.jp
Malaysia	+1-212-316-2000	www.manhattanreview.com
Netherlands	+31-20-808-4399	www.manhattanreview.nl
Philippines	+1-212-316-2000	www.review.ph
Poland	+1-212-316-2000	www.review.pl
Portugal	+1-212-316-2000	www.review.pt
Russia	+1-212-316-2000	www.manhattanreview.ru
Singapore	+65-3158-2571	www.gmat.sg
South Africa	+1-212-316-2000	www.manhattanreview.co.za
South Korea	+1-212-316-2000	www.manhattanreview.kr
Sweden	+1-212-316-2000	www.gmat.se
Spain	+34-911-876-504	www.review.es
Switzerland	+41-435-080-991	www.review.ch
Taiwan	+1-212-316-2000	www.gmat.tw
Thailand	+66-6-0003-5529	www.manhattanreview.com
United Arab Emirates	+1-212-316-2000	www.manhattanreview.ae
United Kingdom	+44-20-7060-9800	www.manhattanreview.co.uk
Rest of World	+1-212-316-2000	www.manhattanreview.com

Contents

Chapter 1

Introduction

Dear Students,

At Manhattan Review, we constantly strive to provide the best educational content for preparation of standardized tests, putting arduous efforts to make things better and better. This continuous evolution is very important for an examination like the GRE, which too evolves constantly. Sadly, a GRE aspirant is confused with too many options in the market. The challenge is how to choose a book or a tutor that prepares you to reach your goal. Without saying that we are the best, we leave it for you to judge.

This book differs in many aspects from standard books available in the market. Unlike Analytical Writing books from other prep companies, this book is comprehensive in many aspects; it includes detailed theory, write-up with an emphasis on how to ideate, detailed 4-step process for two 30-minutes Analytical Writing tasks, template for essay writing, a couple of essays each for issue and argument based essays with four versions (scored 6/5/3/2) and their critiques, a total of 40 essays: 20 argument-based and 20 issue-based, comprehensive list of words, and a collection of quotes to enrich your essays.

In a nut shell, Manhattan Review's GRE-Analytical Writing Guide is holistic and comprehensive in all respects; it is created so because we listen to what students need. Should you have any query, please feel free to write to us at *info@manhattanreview.com*.

Happy Learning!

Prof. Dr. Joern Meissner
& The Manhattan Review Team

Chapter 2

Introduction to GRE Analytical Writing Task

The first section on the GRE is the possibly the one with most polarizing opinions – The Essay Writing Task.

Some people actually look forward to presenting their thoughts on paper while others are terrorized by its thought. However, to master the Essay task, all one needs is structured thinking and a good grasp on English.

GRE Essay is always the first section of the exam, consisting of two essay writing tasks, each for 30 minutes, totaling to 60 minutes in all. The tasks are as follows:

(1) **Analyze an Issue (30 minutes)** – An essay containing your opinion and discussion on a general topic

(2) **Analyze and Argument (30 minutes)** – An essay analyzing the merits and demerits of an argument

The Issue or Argument essays can come in any order but the first section will always be essay writing.

Note that the Essay score is not factored into the general GRE score out of 340. This is a separate score, awarded on a scale of 0 to 6, moving in half-point increments (that is, 0 – 0.5 – 1 – 1.5 ... 5 – 5.5 – 6). Both a computer and a human will evaluate and grade your essay, so you'll receive your Essay score later, when you receive your official scores from ETS, any time within 15 days of your taking the exam. The average score of scores of Issue Task and Argument Task will be your Essay score.

2.1 A brief introduction of the Essay subtypes

2.1.1 The Issue Essay

This task is very similar to academic essays generally written by students as part of their curriculum – the kind that involve 5 or more paragraphs and need the student to state his position on some general topic. The topics contained in the issue range from statements on education or politics to assertions and claims about society and ethics. These will need a student to employ examples from the real world, possibly of world-famous personalities. More important would be the ability to state and cogently develop a particular opinion.

2.1.2 The Argument Essay

This task will present you with a flawed argument and you have to analyze the flaws to discuss them in your essay. In this task, unlike in the previous one, your opinion is irrelevant. The argument contains flaws, which you find and present in a logically compelling manner. Thus, all this essay task needs is a clear way of thinking and approaching an argument and calmly dissecting it and illustrating its flaws. This task will be easier to prepare for than the Issue Task.

2.1.3 How important are the Essay scores?

The Essay Task is not to be taken lightly. First of all, the way you attempt the task, in a smooth or bumpy manner, will set the tone for the rest of your test-taking experience. So, the attempt should be carefully planned and prepared for. Second point is the Essay score. Almost all graduate schools have their specific cut-offs not just for GRE general score (out of 340) but also for the Essay score (out of 6). The cut-offs range from 3.5 (for science-based courses) to 4.5 (for arts-based courses); therefore, you should aim for 4.5 and above to be safe.

Also, ETS (the maker of GRE) goes on record to state "Validity research has shown that Analytical Writing essay score is correlated with academic writing more highly than is the personal statement." What this means is that both ETS and the graduate schools know that the essays written by you in this task are far more accurate representations of your writing and thinking skills than are the application essays presented during admissions. It is a documented fact that you will write your Essay tasks but there is no guarantee that you will write your application essays.

While there's no consensus on how exactly the graduate schools use the essay scores, the possibilities are that since all graduate students need some writing skills most schools want at least an adequate writing capability in their students, and the schools that offer a writing-intensive or thesis-oriented course will heavily depend on the essay scores. Also, many schools use the essay as an elimination criterion. A great Essay score will not necessarily offset your GRE score, especially if the general GRE score (out of 340) is low. However, a bad Essay score (below 4.0) will definitely hamper your chances of admissions, even if you have a superb general GRE score (out of 340). The purpose of Essay is to help graduate schools cull out the bottom 20% of candidates – the ones who cannot write English well-enough to manage graduate-level curriculum, or those who are not structured in their thinking or their approach, or are downright not serious about the process.

To find out what score you exactly need in your essay task, best to contact the admissions department of the graduate school. If they don't provide any specific answers, you have to be safe and acquire 4.5 or higher.

A seemingly scary fact is that schools can choose to read your essay, but it's not necessary that they will. In fact, they most certainly won't, given the amount of work that they have during the admissions process. They may read the essay of those who score low but are still in consideration for a seat. Also, be reassured that the schools know that you have only 30 minutes in which to write the essay and they realize that the essay represents a first draft of sorts. ETS provides a **"Guide to the Use of Scores"**, primarily for university admissions department, in which ETS writes **"A GRE response should be considered a rough first draft since examinees do not have sufficient time to revise their essays during the test. Examinees also do not have dictionaries or spell-checking or grammar-checking software available to them."**

2.1.4   Scoring parameters in the essays

The three main things that the Essay task is scored on are

(1) **Organization and presentation** – How do you present your thoughts: coherently or haphazardly

(2) **Logical analysis** – The quality of your ideas and points: whether the flaws you find are important or flimsy

(3) **Linguistic skills** – The level of your writing: persuasive or flawed

The Essay Task is described on the ETS website. It also includes a description of different scores and some example essays of different scores. The material is worth reading at least once. ETS also provides a complete pool of essay topics from which you will get an essay in your exam, both Issue and Argument.

They can be found at:

http://www.ets.org/gre/revised_general/prepare/analytical_writing/issue/pool

http://www.ets.org/gre/revised_general/prepare/analytical_writing/argument/pool

The number of essays is around 250 or so, but there is no need to practice writing all of them. Once you know how to organize your essay, how to brainstorm for ideas and how to present your thoughts on paper, practice writing some essays and just read the remaining Essay prompts, as well as the Sample Essays in the subsequent chapters. That should be enough for you to get a high score on the Essay section.

Score 6.0 is the highest score you can get on the Essay task. Remember that it is not factored into your general GRE score (out of 340).

To get a score of 6.0, according to ETS, your essay addresses the specific prompt while:

(1) Presenting an insightful position on the issue

(2) Developing the position with compelling reasons and/or persuasive examples

(3) Sustaining a well-focuses, well-organized analysis, connecting ideas logically

(4) Expressing ideas fluently and precisely, using effective vocabulary and sentence variety

(5) Demonstrating facility with the conventions (i.e., grammar, usage, and mechanics) of standard written English, with possibly a few minor errors

In other words, priority is organization and quality of ideas, along with sharp and crisp use of English.

Graders are specially trained college and university faculty. All of your personal details are withheld from them. Each of your two essays will be graded by a reader and an e-rater (a computer program). These scores are averaged to the nearest half-point score. Only if the grades assigned to the essay by the reader and the e-rater differ by more than a point will another reader, a moderator, be assigned to decide on the matter.

The length of the essay

While ETS, or any graduate school generally deny that there is any link between essay score and essay length, the scored essays provided overwhelmingly suggest that most high-scoring essay (5.0 or higher) are far longer than the lower-scoring ones. In other words, statistically, it is far more likely to get a score of 5.0 or higher is your essays contain more than 4 paragraphs, ideally 5 paragraphs. So, aim to do exactly so. Assign one para each for introduction and conclusion, leaving 3 clear body paragraphs containing the "meat" of your discussions. To this end, it is suggested that you ensure that typing 5 paragraphs does not take you longer than 18-20 minutes, since that will be the time available to do so. Check your current typing speed and aim to improve it every time you practice any Essay task.

Linguistics in the essay

Good grammar and spelling are always appreciated. However, don't focus disproportionately on trying to dress up your Essay beyond a certain point.

ETS has quoted "scorers are trained to focus on the analytical logic of the essays more than on spelling, grammar or syntax. The mechanics of writing are weighed in their ratings only to the extent that these impede clarity or meaning." Thus, the ETS states that language is important only as a means of communication. That is, as long as the grader can clearly understand what you tried to convey, marks will not be deducted for use of language. That is not to say that compelling and persuasive language cannot mean the difference between a 5, or 5.5 and 6.0. However, you should focus on language improvement only after you have gotten a complete grip on the essay tasks.

2.2   How does the GRE program operate in the Essay?

Before we get into the actual details of either the Issue Task or the Argument Task, let's take a look at the physical mechanics of the Essay program. A textbox on a part of the screen is the space in which you have to type your essay response. There is no limit to how much text you can enter but the textbox cannot be "resized", that is, once you have entered about 9-11 lines, you will have to scroll up or down to read what you have written. The whole program looks very much like "Notepad" application, with absolutely no formatting functions such as "Bold" or "Italics", etc. You will have "cut", "paste" and "undo" buttons. Don't try to emphasize any particular part of your essay response using All Caps or asterisks or any such keyboard-based trick. Let the sharpness of your essay persuade the reader.

The navigation keys on the keyboard have their standard function for moving the cursor up, down, left, or right. Enter and Return key insert a paragraph break and move you to a new line.

Page Up and Page Down retain their standard function of moving the cursor up or down one screen. The keyboard also allows standard functions of Backspace and Delete buttons, and Home and End buttons too have their functions.

Tab or Indent is not allowed. To make a new paragraph, just press Enter a couple of times to put a black space between paragraphs. If you prefer putting indents at the start of new paragraphs, just hit Space Bar a preset number of times, say 5 times for every new paragraph, to create a consistent indenting effect.

You can use the following keyboard shortcuts, when you are editing your essay.

Combination	Function	Description
Ctrl-X or Alt-T	Cut	Cuts text and puts it on a clipboard
Ctrl-C or Alt-C	Copy	Copies text onto the clipboard
Ctrl-V or Alt-P	Paste	Pastes text from the clipboard
Ctrl-Z or Alt-U	Undo	Undoes the last edit you made (You can undo only your last 10 edits)
Ctrl-Y or Alt-R	Redo	Redoes something you just undid. You can redo only the last 10 undone actions.

Like Notepad, Essay program does not contain a Spell Check option. You have to rely on your own grammar and spelling skills. You would obviously not make any spelling or grammar mistakes deliberately, so, to ensure the fewest number of errors, practice multiple essays in Notepad application to see your spelling mistakes and always carve out the last couple of minutes to edit your essay to weed out the errors.

You will have scratch paper, the same kind that you get (stapled paper-booklet) to use to plan your essay. You could also choose to create an outline in the textbox on screen itself, but be sure to delete any notes before clicking on "Submit". Once you click on "submit", you cannot go back.

Once you have finished the first essay, before or on time, the next essay will begin immediately. You won't get a break between the two essay tasks but you will get a 10-minute break after both the essay tasks are through.

2.3   How to use the 30 minutes?

You are given exactly 30 minutes for each task to do all you can with the particular Essay task given to you. The best way to avoid any unpleasant experience is to have a time-based plan and to stick to it. Here is a plan for each of your 30 minutes:

(1) **2 minutes: Read.** Read the task carefully. Doing so will kick your brain into thinking mode and help you to focus on the task at hand and calm the butterflies in your stomach. In these 2 minutes, read the Essay at least twice to ensure that you don't miss out on any nuance that you can exploit in your essay. In this part, for Argument Essay, you should break down the argument into main conclusion and supporting premises so that you can start work on weakening the assumptions and evidence in the next part.

(2) **5 minutes: Ideate.** Here, you will brainstorm and generate ideas in the manner discussed in Chapter 2 and Chapter 3. This part will generate the main thrust of your essay, so don't rush yourself and stick to the plan. This part should also yield a rough structure of what points you will mention in your essay – the 4 paragraphs. Divide up the ideas into 2 main body paragraphs to allow faster typing in the next part.

(3) **20 minutes: Type.** This part is where you will use the general template discussed in the next chapter and flesh it out using the points you generated in the previous 5 minutes. If you hit a writer's block, don't force yourself to go in a linear fashion. Type out whatever points occur to you and then at every pause, make sure you have arranged the points in proper order. By the end of this part, you should have a draft of your essay. To hit around 500 words, you should have written about 30-35 sentences of 15-20 words each. With sufficient practice, your essays will reach the desirable mark and you would not have to actually count the number of words on the day of your exam.

(4) **3 minutes: Review.** At this point, resist the temptation of adding any new points. Just read your essay twice, correcting it for grammar and spelling mistakes as you read and ensuring that proper transition words have been used as you switched from one point to the next. Also, try to up the vocabulary level but don't try to use language, words or quotes/sayings that you are not completely familiar with.

Stick to formal English and keep the language relevant and unornamented. Use the vocabulary help given at the end of the book.

2.4 General tips

(1) After having read the full book, practice writing at least 4-5 essays.

(2) Make sure you do go through the remaining Essay topics in the pool and think about what you would generally write about them.

(3) In your final 3-4 full-length tests, you should do the Essay part too, to get the full experience.

(4) Check your typing speed – it is better to write essays closer to 550-600 words than just 300 or so words. You should be able to type that many words in less than 20 minutes.

(5) Absorb the vocabulary used in the 40 sample essays provided in the book as well as in the vocabulary section in the next chapter. You should be familiar enough with these to incorporate them into your essay without any hassles.

(6) Read the sample essays more than once to train your mind to think along those lines.

(7) If your command on English is not strong, make sure you adhere to the principles you learnt in high school English. Reading quality publications, such as The New Yorker, phys.org, or aldaily.com, among other things may help you to familiarize yourself with excellent English.

Chapter 3

Analyze an Issue

3.1 What is an Issue?

An Issue is a generalized statement or a claim, on such topics as politics, education, socity, morality, ethics, science and technology, etc.

3.1.1 The Issue Task

This task asks you to present your opinions with reasoning and examples, opinions on a general claim or statement. You can choose to either agree or disagree with the given statement, or even take a balanced view for that matter. You must support all aspects of the position that you choose to take. The topic will be from the ETS Pool of Issue Tasks.

Do note that you are generally expected to pick a side, either "for" or "against", over and above discussing the nitty-gritty's of the issue. However, taking an extreme position is not advisable, that is, do not extremely argue for or against the issue. Acknowledge that all issues have two sides, with both sides having some validity to their claims, even though one side's claims may outweigh the other. Apart from this, follow the specific prompt that is given to you with your Issue statement, because that prompt can determine the extent to which you discuss the other side, or the opposition and its claims.

The prompt you will get with your issue statement will be one of the following six possible prompts.

(1) Write a response in which you discuss the extent to which you agree or disagree with the statement and explain your reasoning for the position you take. In developing and supporting your position, you should consider ways in which the statement might or might not hold true and explain how these considerations shape your position.

(2) Write a response in which you discuss the extent to which you agree or disagree with the recommendation and explain your reasoning for the position you take. In developing and supporting your position, describe specific circumstances in

which adopting the recommendation would or would not be advantageous and explain how these examples shape your position.

(3) Write a response in which you discuss the extent to which you agree or disagree with the claim. In develop-ing and supporting your position, be sure to address the most compelling reasons or examples that could be used to challenge your position.

(4) Write a response in which you discuss which view more closely aligns with your own position and explain your reasoning for the position you take. In developing and supporting your position, you should address both of the views presented above.

(5) Write a response in which you discuss the extent to which you agree or disagree with the claim AND the reason on which that claim is based. (NOTE: For this prompt, the claim will be accompanied by a reason why the claim has been made. You'll need to give your opinion on both.)

(6) Write a response in which you discuss your views on the policy above and explain your reasoning for the position you take. In developing and supporting your position, you should consider the possible consequences of implementing the policy and explain how these consequences shape your position.

3.1.2 Analysis of the prompts

While the wording of these prompts may seem distinct, they fall into three general categories:

(1) Choose a side but reasonably acknowledge the opposition – In these prompts, you must pick your side and properly corroborate it, but you must also state and discuss the validity of your opposition's claims and acknowledge them. [Prompt # 1, 2 3 and 4]

(2) Pick and side and explain your reasons –In this style, you don't have to acknowledge your opposition but you have to elaborate on the primary motivations and reasons that led you to choose the side that you did. Thus, in this style, the justification of your side becomes very important. [Prompt # 5]

(3) Select a side and discuss its implications – In this style, you will have to choose a specific course of action or a side and discuss its consequences and implications. [Prompt # 6]

That being said, the analysis of the scoring essay examples given in The Official Guide to the GRE Revised General Test do not seem to follow the prompts specifically, and yet have gotten a high score. So, it is not necessary to follow the specific instructions given in the prompt, provided you.

(1) Choose a side on the given issue, not necessarily overwhelmingly, but a clear side

(2) Justify your choice using reasons AND relevant examples

(3) Remain reasonable by acknowledging and discussing the opposition's claims too

Let's analyze an issue from the ETS Pool of Issue Topics:

> **In any field of endeavor, it is impossible to make a significant contribution without first being strongly influenced by past achievements within that field.**
>
> *Write a response in which you discuss the extent to which you agree or disagree with the statement and explain your reasoning for the position you take. In developing and supporting your position, you should consider ways in which the statement might or might not hold true and explain how these considerations shape your position.*

<u>**The Issue part:**</u>
"In any field ... that field" – This is the main issue statement with which you have to agree or disagree. Your position will be constructed on this statement.

How to actually analyze all the aspects and dig out the possible discussion points will be covered in the subsequent section, especially in the "How to Ideate" part. For now, let us move on to the prompt part and analyze it.

<u>**The prompt part:**</u>

(1) **"Write a response ... you take"** – This is the main task given to you. So, your primary task is to take a clear position and provide the justification for it, that is, defend it.

(2) **"In developing ... your position"** – This part asks you to acknowledge that your position may not necessarily hold true in all circumstances, and asks you to evaluate such considerations. Thus, it asks you to be reasonable and not take an extreme position.

Thus, you need to take a position, state why you choose that position with reasons and examples, but also explain how your position might not be valid in certain cases.

3.2 How to Ideate

<u>Evaluate the terms</u>
First of all, when you get into the "ideation" part of your time, you should analyze every single word of your issue carefully and judge its implications. Evaluating each word can help you to introduce the issue, as well as conclude it well. It can also help you to decide the the position you want to take.

Let's use the above mentioned issue to see how each word evaluation should be done:

The Issue:

In any field of endeavor, it is impossible to make a significant contribution without first being strongly influenced by past achievements within that field.

The Evaluation

Words of the issue	Any field	Impossible	Significant contribution	first	Strongly influenced	Past achievements	
Analysis	Too extreme; nothing can apply to "any" field. The scope needs to be defined.	Too extreme again; does not allow any possibility of any contribution to any field. Again, the scope needs to be defined	Discuss the term "significant" and the term "achievements". These can be defined based on popularity or on impact, or such. These terms need to be delineated	This is being implied as a mandatory step before anything happens. Again, seems extreme	How strongly? What does "influenced" mean in this context? All these points need to be specified before a position can be taken. Most importantly, the author makes it sound as if getting influenced is a negative thing.	Again, the word "achievements" can be interpreted based on use or fame. Without discussing that, the validity of this issue cannot be taken into account.	After

an analysis of the terms employed in the issue is done, it's time to analyze both sides of the issue.

Why both sides of an issue? Because every prompt used by ETS, either directly or indirectly, asks you to take a reasonable position, and not an extreme one. Also, even after stating and justifying your position, you still have to factor in your opposition and given it due discussion. Also, each side has its specific opposition. Thus, once you find your reasons or points, you just flip it and you will easily find the opposite aspect to it.

Also, note that you don't always have to agree with the issue. In fact, most issue statements are worded in an extreme sort of way, making it difficult to defend them and agree with them.

Let's use the above issue to start creating an "agree/disagree" table for ideation.

The Issue:

In any field of endeavor, it is impossible to make a significant contribution without first being strongly influenced by past achievements within that field.

Agree/Disagree table

Agree	Disagree
Can't do anything considerable without learning about developments up to the current point	Pioneers are present in every field, as are trailblazers.
Eg.–Can't innovate in computers, unless you know how to program, how computers work – all achievements of people before your endeavor	Eg.–Everyone thought it was impossible till US put a man on the moon – nothing in the past to be influenced by.

By ideating on "Agree and "Disagree," you are thinking in both directions. This is particularly important to help you to come up with counter examples. Ideation can work both ways, that is you can get a reason and then find an example on the basis of the reason, or you can think of some example and then pin down its underlying reason.

To fasten the ideation, simply try to think of examples similar to the ones you get in the first round. Once you get an idea like "field of computer science", you can check it for further examples, for either side. For example, you might consider Tim Berners Lee, who invented the World Wide Web – he did not rely on past achievements but made significant contributions of his own. Same would be true of Steve Jobs and Bill Gates. However, other achievements such as Google, would never have been possible without the past achievement of Tim B Lee!

So, the updated table:

Agree/Disagree table

Agree	Disagree
Can't do anything considerable without learning about developments up to the current point	Pioneers are present in every field, as are trailblazers.
Eg.–Can't innovate in computers, unless you know how to program, how computers work – all achievements of people before you	Eg.–Everyone thought it was impossible till US put a man on the moon – nothing in the past to be influenced by.
Google and all other internet of computer-based developments	Tim Berners Lee, Bill Gates, Steve Jobs
You cannot think asymmetrically about any subject until you know what the conventional concepts in that field are. Thus, being influenced by the past knowledge and achievements of the field is necessary for anyone who eventually achieves something big	New concepts and things are discovered when people break off from conventions Eg.–Copernicus, Newton, Pollack, Galileo, Einstein, etc
	Almost everyone who is schooled follows and is influenced by the achievements of the past, but does not end up making considerable contributions because of that necessarily

You can stop as soon as you have 2-3 good ideas for one side.

Notice that the examples above are sourced from history and current events. While personal examples are not prohibited, they don't make for the most convincing essays. That being said, personal examples are better than no examples at all. If you're stuck and can't hit upon anything, better to use personal examples that nothing at all.

If you don't want to use multiple examples in your essay, you can also consider just elaborating on the reasoning part. A well-balanced essay includes the position, properly justified reasoning and examples. So, to reduce the weightage given to examples, just flesh out your reasoning aspect more. Also, don't waste good examples by simply mentioning them. Link the examples to your reasoning by properly describing its connection to your point.

There are many topics that don't lend themselves well to examples, and have to be discussed using only reasoning. The only implementation issue you can face in such situations is how to divide the reasoning up into individual (discrete) packets.

Let's analyze one such Issue sample from the ETS Pool

"Every individual in a society has a responsibility to obey just laws and to disobey and resist unjust laws."

This example does not so much favor examples as reasoning. Most such topics can be neatly chalked up on "agree/disagree" table using the following parameters.

(1) <u>Stakeholder's perspectives</u>: Think of all the possible stakeholders associated with that given issue and analyze the issue from their individual perspectives

(2) <u>Geographical angle</u>: Factor in the location and size, area, density, national, international and economic angles and analyze the impact of the issue

(3) <u>Ethical views</u>: If the issue involves morality, discuss those aspects too

(4) <u>Historical connections</u>: If there are historical aspects to the issue, they should be discussed

(5) <u>Implementation and feasibility</u>: discussing whether the issue deals with potentially executable recommendations (if there is one) is a good idea

Let's draw up an "agree/disagree" table using the above parameters

Parameters	Agree	Disagree	
Stakeholders: individuals, lawmakers, law enforcers, government	Society's upkeep is as much a responsibility of an individual as it is of the government. Thus, if someone in power errs, the individuals should rectify it	Who will hold the power to decide what's "just" and what's "unjust"? With whom in mind will the "justness" of the law be determined? This is impossible to determine	
Implementation and feasibility		If the individuals are given the freedom to ascertain the fairness of the laws, anarchy will descend on the society because every individual will have the incentive to look for vested interests	
Ethical views	If something is unethical, it should be fought against	Fairness is an abstract concept. To execute it in law needs proper knowledge, something that individuals cannot have. Thus, leaving this responsibility to individuals is not logical	Notice
Geographical angle		The bigger the size of the nation, the more interpretations there will be about just and unjust laws. Also, economic activities will be heavily affected by encouraging people to become vigilantes	
Historical	Historically, the people have often waited too long to protest against unfair things	Just because history is full of examples of people successfully revolting against unfair laws does not mean the current scenario warrants it	

that the table is skewed and unbalanced. In fact, it should be so! This gives us a clear side!

The chart above shows five arguments on "disagree" side. You won't have time to write an entire body paragraph about each one, and some ideas are too small to write entire paragraphs on. So, choose your biggest three points of divide up all the points in three body paragraphs and write.

Do remember to briefly mention words from the specific prompt that you get. Just try to incorporate specific words from the prompt in the introduction and conclusion part of the paragraphs and at the beginning and end of the body paragraphs.

Also remember that some issues are such that there won't be a clear side to it. Don't be worried if you find that you have as many points to "agree" as you have to "disagree" with the issue. Take a balanced approach to such issues. However, balanced does not mean vague or ambiguous. Be clear and crisp. Explain each aspect and state how a certain situation makes you agree with the issue while another situation makes you disagree with it. Be direct, and not wishy-washy.

3.2.1 Finally be careful to not be:

Too Extreme: Using words like always, never, only, fully, etc. leaves no room to maneuver and makes for a tight position. This will directly work against being reasonable and being reasonable is the most important instruction in issue prompts.

Too emotional or irrational: Using emotions or pathos to justify your stand will paint you as an irrational creature. Remember to provide logic-based reasons rather than high-sounding, advice-like emotional or mushy statements.

In other words, your position shouldn't be something so extreme that you can't justify it but it also shouldn't be something so routine and boring that everyone would be wont to disagree with it. Don't oversimplify but use a position that you would if you were in an interesting, intelligent discussion with your college admissions committee.

3.2.2 Timing

Your ideation bit should not take you longer than 3-4 minutes. Our table contains far more points than you actually need to make in your actual essay. Also, our table contains full sentences and examples. All you need to make a table in your own shorthand for you to comprehend it. You may even just write the examples and work on the points in your essay. The more you practice the better you will be at it on the exam day!

3.2.3 How to structure the Issue?

Here is a basic structure for the Issue. You can adapt it within the general framework given to you.

Introduction

You can start the essay in any of the following ways

(1) A relevant quote

(2) A global example

(3) A historical background of the main point in the issue

After any of the above, provide a generalized description of the issue topic.

Then, state your position in an unequivocal and unambiguous way – very clearly

Finally, before moving on the body paragraphs, discuss the various aspects by which you will present your position, possibly discuss the scope of the issue.

Body paragraph 1

Use a connector: To begin with...
State your position
Provide detailed reasoning
Link it with a specific and relevant example
Circle back to the point

Body paragraph 2 and 3

Use appropriate connectors and repeat the process given above for body paragraph 1

Conclusion

Connector: To conclude, to sum up, etc.

Briefly recap the points discussed above but in different and general terms.
Restate your position in a general way, possibly discussing the way forward or ending on a positive note.

Some points to remember

(1) Don't start every sentence with "I think" or "I believe" but don't be too formal. Equally, don't try to be funny. Treat this as a formal, academic essay.

(2) Try to vary your vocabulary even when you find yourself repeating the same things. You can keep this exercise for the last 5 minutes of your time slot, exchanging words. Especially try to incorporate the words given to you in the "polishing essay" part.

(3) Use different types of sentences involving different structures. As in simple sentences, complex sentences, inverted ones, rhetorical ones, etc.

(4) Using quotations can instantly add value to your essay but don't use more than two for any essay. One for the introduction and possibly one for the conclusion, only if they are relevant, will suffice. Use the "polishing essay" section to get quotations.

(5) Length is important. Try to make minimum 4 paragraphs in the essay.

(6) When starting the writing aspect in your essay, don't worry about having to start with the introduction first. Once you have finished ideation, start with the body paragraph, or with whichever section on which the ideas flow. You can always add the introduction later.

Chapter 4

Analyze an Argument

4.1   What is an argument?

An argument is a logic-based (but flawed) proposition or recommendation, made by an author, who provides some conclusion or claim on the basis of some premise, typically, data, situation, or considerations. The argument presented in the form of a short passage

4.2   The Argument Task

The Analyze an Argument task involves writing a critique of the given argument in 30. A critique of any point other than that in the argument will receive a score of zero. To get a good score, you need to do three things:

(1) Analyze the line of reasoning in the argument (which will never be sound).

(2) Discuss the main flaws and faulty assumptions that underlie that reasoning.

(3) Recommend what the author could do to make the conclusion of the argument sound.

Note that, unlike the Analyze an Issue Task, in this task your opinions are irrelevant. The only relevant and important thing is a proper evaluation of the given argument.

From the previous chapter, you already know what the Essay specifically grades you on. Now let's get into an actual Argument Essay to understand how to write it.

Let's look at an actual example from the Argument Pool.

The following appeared as a letter to the editor from a Central Plaza store owner.

"Over the past two years, the number of shoppers in Central Plaza has been steadily decreasing while the popularity of skateboarding has increased dramatically. Many Central Plaza store owners believe that the decrease in their business is due to the

---

number of skateboard users in the plaza. There has also been a dramatic increase in the amount of litter and vandalism throughout the plaza. Thus, we recommend that the city prohibit skateboarding in Central Plaza. If skateboarding is prohibited here, we predict that business in Central Plaza will return to its previously high levels."

Write a response in which you discuss what questions would need to be answered in order to decide whether the recommendation is likely to have the predicted result. Be sure to explain how the answers to these questions would help to evaluate the recommendation.

ETS lists eight possible prompts, any one of which could follow the Argument in the task. This is done to prevent any sort of pre-exam preparation of the Essays, but sadly is ineffectual because while the wording of the prompts may differ, the actual essence barely changes. However, you must note the specific wording of the given prompt and try to incorporate those words into the introduction and conclusion parts of your essay.

(1) Write a response in which you discuss what specific evidence is needed to evaluate the argument and explain how the evidence would weaken or strengthen the argument.

(2) Write a response in which you examine the stated and/or unstated assumptions of the argument. Be sure to explain how the argument depends on these assumptions and what the implications are if the assumptions prove unwarranted.

(3) Write a response in which you discuss what questions would need to be answered in order to decide whether the recommendation and the argument on which it is based are reasonable. Be sure to explain how the answers to these questions would help to evaluate the recommendation.

(4) Write a response in which you discuss what questions would need to be answered in order to decide whether the advice and the argument on which it is based are reasonable. Be sure to explain how the answers to these questions would help to evaluate the advice.

(5) Write a response in which you discuss what questions would need to be answered to decide whether the re-commendation is likely to have the predicted result. Be sure to explain how the answers to these questions would help to evaluate the recommendation.

(6) Write a response in which you discuss what questions would need to be answered in order to decide whether the prediction and the argument on which it is based are reasonable. Be sure to explain how the answers to these questions would help to evaluate the prediction.

(7) Write a response in which you discuss one or more alternative explanations that could rival the proposed explanation and explain how your explanation(s) can plausibly account for the facts presented in the argument.

(8) Write a response in which you discuss what questions would need to be addressed in order to decide whether the conclusion and the argument on which it is based are reasonable. Be sure to explain how the answers to the questions would help to evaluate the conclusion.

Analysis of the prompts

All the prompts ask you to find faults with the given argument, thus proving that any possible argument from the ETS Pool of Argument Essays will be flawed. Thus, your basic task is to find the flaws in the given argument. While the prompts use words such as evidence, counter-explanations, assumptions, questions, etc, all these are mere smokescreens that all imply that you should find 1) faulty assumptions on which the argument is based, and 2) the missing evidence that should have been provided by the author. Along with these two main things, also use counter-examples that weaken the author's point to support your claims. Finally, add some recommendations to remedy the given flaws.

Do not be daunted by the seemingly different construction of the prompt. All you have to do to score well is write a well-constructed essay, pinpointing the logical flaws in the argument and mentioning possible remedies to correct those flaws. That is not to say that you can ignore the specific instructions altogether. Read them and make sure that they are addressed to improve your score.

Let's analyze an argument from the ETS Pool of Argument Topics:

The following appeared as a letter to the editor from a Central Plaza store owner.

"Over the past two years, the number of shoppers in Central Plaza has been steadily decreasing while the popularity of skateboarding has increased dramatically. Many Central Plaza store owners believe that the decrease in their business is due to the number of skateboard users in the plaza. There has also been a dramatic increase in the amount of litter and vandalism throughout the plaza. Thus, we recommend that the city prohibit skateboarding in Central Plaza. If skateboarding is prohibited here, we predict that business in Central Plaza will return to its previously high levels."

Write a response in which you discuss what questions would need to be answered in order to decide whether the recommendation is likely to have the predicted result. Be sure to explain how the answers to these questions would help to evaluate the recommendation.

<u>The argument part:</u>

(1) "The following appeared ... store owner" – This part tells us from where the argument has been picked up. We can use this info bit into the wording of the essay.

Instead of saying "the argument states this… or that" we can state "The letter …" or "The store owner …". You should be aware of where the argument has been picked from to understand its context.

(2) "Over the past … dramatically" – This is a premise, a fact, in the given argument. Based on this data, the store owner has made a claim.

(3) "Many Central Plaza … in the plaza" – This too is another premise, a piece of support used by the store owner to substantiate his claim. He is using the force of collective (many store owners…) to drive in his point.

(4) "There has been … the plaza" – This is yet another premise employed by the store owner to add weight to his claim. He is using shock value(dramatic increase…) to make his point

(5) "Thus, we recommend … Plaza" – This is the primary claim or conclusion made by the announcement/argument. The validity of this is doubtful because it is based on incomplete evidence and flawed assumptions.

(6) "If skateboarding … high levels" – This is an additional claim made by the argument/announcement. Since this claim too is based on the same incomplete evidence and faulty assumptions, it is flawed and unsound too.

How to actually analyze the faulty assumptions and dig out the missing evidence will be covered in the subsequent section, especially in the "How to Ideate" part. For now, let us move on to the prompt part and analyze it.

The prompt part:

The prompt given for any argument remains the same. Let's analyze it sentence by sentence.

(1) *Write a response in which you discuss what questions would need to be answered in order to decide whether the recommendation is likely to have the predicted result*– This part is a general instruction that we have to write an essay that discusses the logic and reasoning of the given argument. So, the primary task is to pin down and cogently explain the questions that need to be answered to judge whether the recommendation will achieve its goal, thus implying that there is evidence that needs to be provided, logic that needs to be assessed and questions that need to be answered.

(2) *Be sure to explain how the answers to these questions would help to evaluate the recommendation* – This part asks us to explain how the specific data we find by asking questions (as per sentence 1 of this prompt) will be relevant. Thus, this part implies that we need to support the claims you make, and the questions you ask by providing the logic behind it and possible presenting counter-explanations that prompt you to ask the questions you ask.

Thus, we need to evaluate the argument, explains why its reasoning is faulty and use of evidence insufficient and then explain how to deal with those issues to make the argument stronger.

The argument provided is never strong. It always contains flaws.

Let's take a look at the two basic parameters provided by the prompt: line of reasoning and use of evidence. We will analyze what they mean.

Line of reasoning

This aspect pertains to the way the argument has been constructed, that is, whether the main conclusion is based on assumptions and whether those assumptions are warranted. To analyze the line of reasoning, think following:

(1) Is the main conclusion the based on assumptions?

(2) What are the assumptions?

(3) Are these assumptions justified?

(4) Why aren't the assumptions justified?

(5) What data could help to evaluate the assumptions? (at this point your thoughts will cross over to the "use of evidence" part)

Use of evidence

This aspect is linked to the assumptions part. The fact is that because use of evidence is insufficient to rove the main conclusion, the conclusion is said to rely on unwarranted assumptions. Thus, for every unjustified assumption you pin down, you will find that related data is missing, and that the data needs to be incorporated to make the claim valid. Ask yourself:

(1) Is the main conclusion the only possible interpretation of the evidence?

(2) What alternative interpretations are possible?

(3) What evidence should have been given to negate the alternative interpretations?

(4) What evidence would have addressed the faulty assumptions?

(5) What could have the author provided to prove what he wishes to prove?

Note that your task is not to agree or disagree with the author. You have to critique the argument – provides its main weaknesses and explain them. You can choose to discuss how to strengthen that claim. However, your primary concern should be the major flaws in the argument and their explanations.

4.3 How to Ideate

To generate ideas to write your essay, first remember that you need ideas along a set pattern, that is,

---

Find a flaw

⇓

Identify its underlying assumption

⇓

Identify the relevant requisite evidence to deal with it.

Sticking to this pattern will keep your thinking structured in the ideation part. Also, even if you don't adhere to the actual series, and end up achieving, say, the second or the third step (find an assumption or missing evidence), you can still find its associated flaw. Don't be finicky about how you think and in which order as long as you get the creative juices flowing!

As the first step, you should analyze the argument, sentence by sentence. A trick to understand the argument and its flaws better is to take each sentence and rephrase it mentally. That may show you how it is meant to serve as proof. At each premise, ask yourself whether it is sufficient to prove the claim and what facts is the premise taking for granted? What else should the author have said besides that premise? What can strengthen that premise? When you reach the claim, ask yourself whether it is justified and what other information would you require?

On your scratch paper you can have a mini table of the following sort to keep track of your thoughts and later on apportion sections of it to specific body paragraphs.

Line #	Sufficient?	Assumption?	More proof?	Flaw?	Counter?
1	N	...	...	...	...
2	N	...	...	...	...

Let's try this method on the argument given above.

The following appeared as a letter to the editor from a Central Plaza store owner.

"Over the past two years, the number of shoppers in Central Plaza has been steadily decreasing while the popularity of skateboarding has increased dramatically. Many Central Plaza store owners believe that the decrease in their business is due to the number of skateboard users in the plaza. There has also been a dramatic increase in the amount of litter and vandalism throughout the plaza. Thus, we recommend

---

that the city prohibit skateboarding in Central Plaza. If skateboarding is prohibited here, we predict that business in Central Plaza will return to its previously high levels."

Line #	Sufficient?	Assumption?	More proof?	Flaw?	Counter?
1 – Premise	No	The decrease in either number is significant	Specific data on the number of shoppers and skateboarders	Skateboarders are not customers who can replace the decreasing number of shoppers	What if skateboarders are legitimate shoppers too? What if the decrease in number of shoppers is insignificant?
2 – Premise	No	Skateboarders are directly responsible for the decrease in number of shoppers	Specific data proving that the decrease in number of shoppers is caused by increase in number of skateboarders	Increasing number of skateboarders led to decreasing number of shoppers	What if some other factor led to the decrease in number of shoppers?
3 – Premise	No	Skateboarders are responsible for litter and vandalism	Specifics linking skateboarders to littering and vandalism	Increase in number of skateboarders led to increase in litter and vandalism	What if some other factor is responsible for increase in litter and vandalism?
4 – Main claim	No	Skateboarders are the problem	Proof asked for above to link skateboarders to these issues	Assumed the truth of the conclusion yet to be proved	What if skateboarders are a significant portion of the mall shoppers?

5 – Additional claim	No	Skateboarders are not responsible for any part of the revenue	Data showing whether skateboarders are an important part of revenue	Assumed the cause and effect yet to be proved. Assumed that skateboarders and shoppers are mutually exclusive	What if some other factor reduced the number of shoppers?

The line by line method will probably not yield the flaw. To understand the kind of flaws that are present, go through the commonest flaws table that follows. Study it thoroughly and learn to identify these flaws in the subsequent sample essays and the remaining Essay arguments from the pool. These flaws recur constantly. In fact, these flaws make up the flaws present in almost all the arguments.

	Faulty Assumption	Required Relevant evidence
Assumed positive correlation as cause and effect	The author assumes that both X and Y underwent changes, so X must be the cause of Y	How is X specifically the direct cause of Y?
Assumed no alternative cause	The author assumes that only X has caused Y without considering alternative causes	Whether there are alternative possible causes? How is only X responsible for Y?
Assumed related because of sequence	X happened before Y, or Y happened after X; therefore, X caused Y, just because they happened one after another	How does the sequence prove that X caused Y? What are other possible factors?
Assumed representative data	The author provides sample data and assumes that it is representative	Whether the data is representative and how specifically so?
Vague terminology	The author assumes things are important by use of vague or extreme terminology	Specific data rather than terms and generalizations

Assumed percents are significant in numbers	The author provides data in percents and assumes that it is significant in numbers too, or provides data in numbers and assumes it is significant overall	What is the entire picture? The data in both numbers and percents
Assumed future based on past	The author provides past performance and assumes it would be so in the future	How would that performance be repeated? Specifics about the plans. Past performance is only indicative not predictive
Assumed necessary	The author assumes that something is needed without stating why	What should he have provided to prove it is needed?
Assumed justified	The author does not give logical reasons for why a particular thing is needed	What reasons instead he should have given with what evidence?
Assumed viable	The author does not give the cost-benefit analysis/financials of the whole recommendation or contingency plans	Should have given specific financial plan details
Assumed compliance	The author fails to mention all stakeholders' position, and has assumed that everyone will be okay	He should have provided details of impact on all stakeholders and specific plan on how to deal with/minimize the impact
Assumed comparable	The author compares two entities without first establishing that they are comparable	Should have specified how exactly they are comparable

4.4 How to Structure the Essay?

The basic structure for any formal essay includes three elements:

(1) Introduction

(2) Body

(3) Conclusion

4.4.1   The Introduction [4 sentences, max]

(1)   Sum up the argument briefly and in general. This always serves as a good anchor and ensures that there is no writing block that you suffer from. You can begin with "The argument claims that ..." Remember to just generally mention, without judgment, the main point and its basis. Don't end up repeating the entire argument. Use a couple of sentences at the most for this step.

(2)   Next point in the intro is to state your position in a general way. You can state that the argument is weak because it relies on faulty line of reasoning and lack of evidence. Use a couple of sentences, if needed. Even one sentence is fine.

(3)   Sum up the flaws in general. Present a sentence that briefly introduces the flaws you wish to pinpoint. You can use the flaw titles from the above table of fallacies.

4.4.2   The Body [2-3 paragraphs]

Choose 3-5 big flaws at the most and divide it up into 2-3 big body paragraphs. Don't try to write all the possible flaws. Choose the big flaws and explain them well.

Body paragraph 1

(1)   Use a connector to highlight transition from intro to first body paragraph: To begin with, to start with, the main issue is, the primary flaw is, etc

(2)   State what the author has stated that you are about to attack. [1 sentence]

(3)   State your position on the sentence and the reason – for example "The author's claim seems highly unlikely because ..." [1 sentence]

(4)   Explain why. You have provided a reason in the previous sentence. Now spend a couple of sentences explaining with the help of an example. You can use an alternative scenario as an example. For instance "Consider the scenario that ..." [2 sentences]

(5)   Circle back to your point. Reinstate how the reason you provided in point 2 made the claim weak – "This possibility proves that the conclusion is vulnerable" [1 sentence]

(6)   State the next flaw and repeat steps 2-5. [3 sentences]

Body paragraph 2

(1)   _Use a connector to highlight transition from first body paragraph to the second: Furthermore, Moreover, Another issue is, A secondary problem is, etc

(2)   Repeat steps 2-6, as given in the body paragraph 1, with new points.

4.4.3   The Conclusion [4 sentences, max]

The conclusion serves to sum up the essay and to make recommendations to the author. Don't make any new points, or discuss new flaws.

(1) Recommendations – State what the author could have done to make his argument stronger and to deal with the flaws you highlighted in the two body paragraphs [2-3 sentences]

(2) Final position – simply state in general that because the given argument contains the given flaws, it is weak and unsound.

Chapter 5

Polishing the essays

5.1 Improving vocab and language

To improve the language of the essay and to distinguish it, you need to use appropriate and sharp vocabulary. Therefore, we have a table of vocabulary for you to use.

Instead of this	Use this
Conclusion	Claim, prediction, recommendation, proposition, assertion, declaration, affirmation, contention, outcome, position, opinion, judgment, decision, culmination, conviction, belief, inference, deduction
The author states	The writer posits, claims, postulates, proposes, asserts, predicates, propounds, puts forth, declares, expresses, affirms, maintains, contends
The author suggests	The author implies, extrapolates, deduces, intimates, offers as consideration, evokes, indirectly indicates, hints, alludes, connotes, signifies
Faulty	Flawed, defective, inadequate, imperfect, blemished, impaired, inaccurate
Not enough	Insufficient, partial, meagre, deficient
Provide	Furnish, supplement, produce, supply, equip, offer, present, reveal
Weak	Vulnerable, lacking, fallible, unsupported, unjustified, unreinforced, ineffectual, irresolute, unprotected, defenceless, untenable, unviable, unconvincing, unsatisfactory, invalid, flimsy, inconclusive, feeble, unsound, undependable, unstable, not well-founded, fallacious, erroneous, specious, illogical, unreliable
Analysis	Evaluation, study, dissection, estimation, interpretation, judgment, opinion, examination, scrutiny, scanning, perusal, investigation

Support	Bolster, advocate, aid, defend, corroborate, uphold, boost, sustain, prop, shore up, substantiate, authenticate, lend credence to, verify, attest to, defend, fortify, secure, cement, supplement, reassert, underpin
Weaken	Undermine, hinder, handicap, exacerbate, impair, thwart, subvert, injure, compromise, debilitate, threaten, discredit
Prove	Validate, certify, confirm, authenticate, affirm, warrant, establish, demonstrate, ascertain, establish, verify, testify, evince
Analyze	Inspect, scrutinize, peruse, parse through, judge, evaluate
Explain	Rationalize, clarify, justify, define, explicate, illustrate, unravel, delineate, articulate
Argue against	Rebut, contend, dispute, contest, challenge, controvert, negate, belie, oppose
Vague/unclear	Ambiguous, equivocal, obscure, abstruse, impenetrable, incomprehensible ill-defined
Improve	Amend, reconstruct, redress, overcome, ameliorate, augment, upgrade, enhance, polish, temper, refine, elevate, hone
Assume	Presume, presuppose, take from granted,
Emphasize	Underscore, highlight, pinpoint, accentuate, stress, underline, insist, foreground, prioritize
Strengthened	Cogent, conclusive, convincing, compelling, effective, potent, sound, infallible, valid,
Misleading	Deceptive, specious, disingenuous, dissembling, duplicitous
Evidence	Grounds, data, substantiation, demonstration, manifestations

5.2 Connectors/Transitions to employ in the essay

Function	Words/Phrases
To make the first point	To begin with, first off, the main point is, the primary flaw is, the biggest fallacy
To add another point	Additionally, furthermore, moreover, also, similarly, again, apart from this, besides this point
To give examples	For instance, say, suppose, if, consider the case that, a possible scenario is, such as, in particular, namely, particularly, specifically, including, as an illustration, as an example, illustrated with, to list, to enumerate, to detail, to specify
To conclude	To sum up, therefore, thus, as a result, consequently, in conclusion, in final consideration, hence, so
To suggest cause or effect	Because, accordingly, so, pertinently, for this purpose, for this reason, as a basis, it follows
To emphasize	Indeed, especially, most importantly, above all, chiefly, particularly, singularly, truly, in fact, to emphasize

To compare	Similarly, comparatively, coupled with, correspondingly, accompanied by, likewise, in a similar fashion, analogically, in like manner, analogous to, comparable to, considering similar circumstances
To contrast	However, nevertheless, nonetheless, notwithstanding, despite, in spite of, yet, conversely, instead of, on the other hand, on the contrary, rather, while this may be true
To state exceptions	Aside from, apart from, barring, besides, except, excluding, exclusive of, other than, outside of, save
To restate	In other words, point in fact, or, in essence, that is, to say, in short, in brief, to put it differently
To provide a sequence	At first, first of all, to begin with, in the first place, at the same time, for now, for the time being, the next step, in time, in turn, later on, meanwhile, next, then, soon, the meantime, later, while, earlier, simultaneously, afterward, in conclusion, with this in mind, After, afterward, before, then, once, next, last, at last, at length, first, second, etc., at first, formerly, rarely, usually, another, finally, soon, meanwhile, at the same time, for a minute, hour, day, during the morning, day, week, etc., most important, later, ordinarily, to begin with, afterwards, generally, in order to, subsequently, previously, in the meantime, immediately, eventually, concurrently, simultaneously
To summarize	After all, all in all, all things considered, briefly, by and large, in any case, in any event, in brief, in conclusion, on the whole, in short, in summary, in the final analysis, in the long run, on balance, to sum up, to summarize, finally
To concede	Although, at any rate, at least, still, thought, even though, granted that, while it may be true, in spite of, of course

Apart from this, note that using SMS language or contractions (such as can't, don't, won't) is not recommended. Try to use formal writing but equally don't use stiff or awkward language (such as "shall, so as to, in order to")

A collection of quotes according to themes

To instantly raise the level of your issue essay is to add a relevant and specific quote. The following quotes have been sorted according to themes and for their relevance to the GRE issue topics. Memorize a few from every theme and you shouldn't have problems fitting a couple of these into your issue on the day of your exam!

Try to use at least one quote per issue essay you write. However, don't try to force fit. Use a quote only if it works for the specific issue you are writing on.

Education

Calvin Coolidge (30th U.S. President, advocate of small government):

- The world is full of educated derelicts.

Albert Einstein:

- Any intelligent fool can make things bigger, more complex, and more violent. It takes a touch of genius and a lot of courage to move in the opposite direction.

Oscar Wilde (Irish writer and prominent aesthete):

- The public have an insatiable curiosity to know everything. Except what is worth knowing.

Camille Paglia (modern-day American author, professor, dissident feminist):

- Education has become a prisoner of contemporaneity. It is the past, not the dizzy present, that is the best door to the future.,

Socrates (ancient Greek philosopher, teacher of Plato):

- The only good is knowledge and the only evil is ignorance.

Nelson Mandela:

- Education is the most powerful weapon which you can use to change the world

Aristotle:

- The roots of education are bitter, but the fruits are sweet

John Dewey:

- Education is not preparation for life, education is life itself

Allan Bloom:

- Education is the movement from darkness to light
Benjamin Franklin:

- An investment in knowledge pays the best interest

Franklin D Roosevelt:

- Democracy cannot succeed unless those who express their choice are prepared to choose wisely. The real safeguard of democracy, therefore, is education.

Politics/Government

Thomas Jefferson:

The will of the people is the only legitimate foundation of any government, and to protect its free expression should be our first object.

John F. Kennedy (35ᵗʰ U.S. President):

• Efforts and courage are not enough without purpose and direction.

Ronald Reagan:

• Government exists to protect us from each other.

• As government expands, liberty contracts

Gerald Ford:

• A government big enough to give you everything you want is a government big enough to take from you everything you have.

Plutarch:

• An imbalance between the rich and the poor is the oldest and most fatal ailment of all republics

Alexis de Tocqueville:

• The health of a democratic society may be measured by the quality of the functions performed by its private citizens.

Unknown:
• Democracy is a government where you can say what you think even if you don't think

Science

Louis Pasteur:

• Science knows no country, because knowledge belongs to humanity, and is the torch which illuminates the world. Science is the highest personification of the nation because that nation will remain the first which carries the furthest the works of thought and intelligence.

Carl Sagan:

• Science is a way of thinking much more than it is a body of knowledge.

• Edwin Powell Hubble: Equipped with his five senses, man explores the universe around him and calls the adventure Science.

Robert A. Heinlein:

• Everything is theoretically impossible, until it is done.

Stephen Hawking:

• Scientists have become the bearers of the torch of discovery in our quest for knowledge.

George Bernard Shaw:

• Science never solves a problem without creating ten more.

Ralph Waldo Emerson:

• Bad times have a scientific value. These are occasions a good learner would not miss.

Isaac Asimov:

• The saddest aspect of life right now is that science gathers knowledge faster than society gathers wisdom.

Albert Einstein:

• No amount of experimentation can ever prove me right; a single experiment can prove me wrong.

Thomas Huxley:

• Science is simply common sense at its best, that is, rigidly accurate in observation, and merciless to fallacy in logic.

Dan Brown:

• Science and religion are not at odds. Science is simply too young to understand.

Christopher Hitchens:

• That which can be asserted without evidence, can be dismissed without evidence.

Marie Curie:

• Nothing in life is to be feared, it is only to be understood. Now is the time to understand more, so that we may fear less.

Neil deGrasse Tyson:

• The good thing about science is that it's true whether or not you believe in it.

Leadership

Virgil (classical Roman poet):

• Who asks whether the enemy were defeated by strategy or valor?

Mohandas Gandhi (political and spiritual leader of Indian Independence Movement):

• I suppose leadership at one time meant muscles; but today it means getting along with people.

Ralph Waldo Emerson:

• Our chief want is someone who will inspire us to be what we know we could be.

John C. Maxwell:

• Leadership is not about titles, positions or flowcharts. It is about one life influencing another.

• Leaders must be close enough to relate to others, but far enough ahead to motivate them.

Marie Lu:

• If you want to rebel, rebel from inside the system. That's much more powerful than rebelling outside the system.

Peter F. Drucker:

• Management is doing things right; leadership is doing the right things.

Aristotle:

- He who cannot be a good follower cannot be a good leader.

Albert Schweitzer:

- Example is not the main thing in influencing others. It is the only thing.

Steve Jobs:

- Be a yardstick of quality. Some people aren't used to an environment where excellence is expected.

John F. Kennedy:

- Leadership and learning are indispensable to each other.

Rosalynn Carter:

- A leader takes people where they want to go. A great leader takes people where they don't necessarily want to go, but ought to be.

Society

Calvin Coolidge (30th U.S. President, advocate of small government):

- The slogan 'Press on' has solved and always will solve the problems of the human race.

Samuel Beckett (Irish avant-garde writer, highly minimalist, known for bleak outlook):

- The tears of the world are a constant quality. For each one who begins to weep, somewhere else another stops.

Oscar Wilde (Irish writer and prominent aesthete):

- The public have an insatiable curiosity to know everything. Except what is worth knowing.

- Democracy means simply the bludgeoning of the people by the people for the people.

- Discontent is the first step in the progress of a man or a nation.

Camille Paglia (modern-day American author, professor, dissident feminist):

- Popular culture is the new Babylon, into which so much art and intellect now flow.

Ethics, Human Values and Morality

Albert Einstein:

• Two things are infinite: the universe and human stupidity, and I'm not sure about the universe.

Samuel Beckett (Irish avant-garde writer, highly minimalist, known for bleak outlook):

• We lose our hair, our teeth! Our bloom, our ideals.

Martin Luther King, Jr.:

• He who passively accepts evil is as much involved in it as he who helps to perpetrate it.

• Freedom is never voluntarily given by the oppressor; it must be demanded by the oppressed.

• Everybody can be great... because anybody can serve. Injustice anywhere is a threat to justice everywhere.

Voltaire (French Enlightenment writer, philosopher, advocate of civil liberties):

• As long as people believe in absurdities they will continue to commit atrocities. It is hard to free fools from the chains they revere.

• I disapprove of what you say, but I will defend to the death your right to say it.

• It is dangerous to be right when the government is wrong.

Theodore Roosevelt (26th U.S. President):

• Far and away the best prize that life offers is the chance to work hard at work worth doing.

Woodrow Wilson (28th U.S. President, leading intellectual of the Progressive era):

• No nation is fit to sit in judgment upon any other nation.

Ralph Waldo Emerson (19th century American transcendentalist author, proponent of individualism):

• It is said that the world is in a state of bankruptcy, that the world owes the world more than the world can pay.

• Can anything be so elegant as to have few wants, and to serve them one's self?

Socrates (ancient Greek philosopher, teacher of Plato):

- Life contains but two tragedies. One is not to get your heart's desire; the other is to get it.

- The only good is knowledge and the only evil is ignorance.

- From the deepest desires often comes the deadliest hate.

- I am not an Athenian, nor a Greek, but a citizen of the world. Nothing is to be preferred before justice.

- Let him that would move the world, first move himself.

Henry David Thoreau (transcendentalist writer, author of Walden):

- The mass of men lead lives of quiet desperation.

Mohandas Gandhi (political and spiritual leader of Indian Independence Movement):

- God comes to the hungry in the form of food.

- Non-cooperation with evil is as much a duty as is cooperation with good.

Chapter 6

Argument Essays

6.1 Essay 1 (Palean baskets)

> Woven baskets characterized by a particular distinctive pattern have previously been found only in the immediate vicinity of the prehistoric village of Palea and therefore were believed to have been made only by the Palean people. Recently, however, archaeologists discovered such a "Palean" basket in Lithos, an ancient village across the Brim River from Palea. The Brim River is very deep and broad, and so the ancient Paleans could have crossed it only by boat, and no Palean boats have been found. Thus it follows that the so-called Palean baskets were not uniquely Palean.
>
> *Write a response in which you discuss what specific evidence is needed to evaluate the argument and explain how the evidence would weaken or strengthen the argument.*

Understand the argument

The above argument states that what were up to now thought to be Palean baskets cannot be thought of as uniquely Palean anymore. The author supports this claim by stating that one "Palean" basket was found in Lithos, even though up to now such woven baskets with this distinctive pattern have only been found in the immediate vicinity of the prehistoric village of Palea. The author explains that the "Palean" basket found in Lithos has to be of Lithos because Lithos and Palea are separated by Brim River, which is very deep and broad and can be crossed only by boats. However, no Palean boats have been found yet.

Conclusion: Palean baskets were not uniquely Palean.

Faulty assumptions

- One basket is proof enough to make a claim

- No other way the basket could have ended up at Lithos

- Brim River was always deep and board and only crossable by boat

43

- No Palean boat found yet is the same as no Palean boat ever existed

- Lithos could not have made boats

- No other way Paleans could have travelled to Lithos or vice versa

Missing evidence

- Conclusive proof that neither Paleans nor Lithoseans ever made any boat

- Proof that Brim River was always crossable only by boat

- Proof that the basket has been made by people of Lithos

- Proof that there was no contact between the people of Palea and of Lithos

Counter-examples

- What if the one basket ended up in Lithos through some flood or such freak incident?

- What if Paleans had boats but those haven't been found yet?

- What if Lithos people had boats with which they traded with Palea?

- What if some third party traded with both Palea and Lithos?

- What is Brim River wasn't always so deep and broad but was easily crossable earlier?

- What if a bridge had been constructed earlier but has completely disintegrated by now?

Once you have pinned down at least a couple of flaws and their relevant missing evidence, as well as created a few counter-examples to weaken the argument's conclusion, start writing the essay. New points may occur to you as you construct your essay, but incorporate them into your essay only if they blend in with your analysis so far. Resist the urge to include too many points; overkill spoils a sharp essay. However, important points related to the primary structure of the argument must always be included in the essay.

Sample Essay (Score 6)

The author has made a rather bold claim that "Palean baskets", supposedly so, should not be considered exclusively "Palean" any longer. The author has backed his claim up with varied pieces of evidence. While the assorted pieces of evidence do seemingly buttress the claim, unfortunately, they do not paint a complete picture, consequently rendering the argument invalid.

The primary issue with the claim is that it attempts to refute the prevalent belief using a single basket found askew as evidence. Why should one Palean basket found in Lithos outweigh the many others that have been found in the vicinity of Palea so far? There are numerous ways that a basket may have ended up in Lithos, even if we were to assume that the Brim River prevented any contact between Palea and Lithos, ways such as a rampaging flood that may have left contents of either side scattered about on the other side. However, one cannot truly ignore the possibility of the Brim River being crossed by people from both sides. One piece of evidence cited by the author is that the Brim River is very deep and broad, and could be crossed only by boat. The author seems to have not taken geological considerations into account, given that geological changes could have easily made the river wide later on, or change its course earlier. Even assuming this is not so, the author has mistaken absence of evidence for evidence. Palean boats haven't been found does not mean that there weren't any ever. Also, the argument seems suspiciously quiet about the possibility of boats made by people of Lithos. The notion that rivers can be crossed by other means, such as bridges, or through shallower parts of the river hasn't been dealt with either in the argument. Unless concrete evidence is provided, evidence such as scrolls from either Palea or Lithos proving that the Brim River prevented contact and no boats were ever made, nor any other form of crossing the river ever practiced, or that Lithos made "Palean" baskets too, the claim stands weakened. Even if the evidence cited were completely true, what if people from a third village served as points of contact between Palea and Lithos. The alternative possibilities are innumerable!

In conclusion, the author makes an absurd argument using a patch-work of vested evidence. If the author has not withheld the complete picture and provided information about the issues discussed above, the argument would have seemed less far-fetched than it is now.

Explanation of score 6

The given essay response is brilliant in its incisive logic, skilled organization and masterful use of language, especially given the time constraints. The introduction concisely sums up the conclusion and explains crisply why the evidence to make the claim is insufficient.

The body paragraph clearly starts with the biggest flaw and unfolds all the logical flaws in decreasing order of importance. Each of the points has been developed thoroughly and sufficient supports have been used. The conclusion is sharp and sums up the critique well, by explaining why the argument is invalid. The ideas display sharp insight and are logically compelling (single basket as primary evidence, lack of evidence being treated as evidence) and the development is gradual and complex. There are no holes in the thought process. Precise transitions have been used throughout the essay [the primary issue, why, even if, one piece of evidence, given that, assuming this is not so, the notion that, unless, in conclusion, etc.].

The use of language is excellent, displaying a superb level of dexterity with the written language. The essay writer clearly has an adept grip on the conventions of the written language and displays impressive facility with the vocabulary as well. The variety in precise words — buttress, rendering, rampaging, innumerable, far-fetched, etc.

The sentence variety – "While the assorted pieces ... rendering the argument invalid", "Why should one ... of Palea so far?", "Unless concrete evidence ... the claim stands weakened", etc.

All in all, superb work, deserving of score 6.

Sample Essay (Score 5)

The argument claims because a "Palean basket" was found in Lithos, these baskets cannot be categorized as uniquely "Palean" anymore. The argument provides some evidence to support this claim. However, a deeper analysis shows that the evidence does not add up to the conclusion the argument makes, and lacks critical information.

The biggest flaw with the argument is that the entire claim is based upon a single basket that was found in Lithos instead of in Palea. A single basket does not make a convincing argument. That basket could have ended up in Lithos in a multitude of ways! It could have been moved even long after both Palea and Lithos are gone, by some other archaeologist and accidentally left at the wrong place! Such happenings are not uncommon. Furthermore, the author states that because Brim River is very deep and broad, and could be crossed only by boat, and Palean boats haven't been found, there has been no exchange between Palea and Lithos. However, what if Paleans had wooden boats that have degenerated over time and therefore aren't found? Additionally, since the author does not mention Lithos in this aspect, the possibility of boats being made by people of Lithos remains open, weakening the claim. Also, it's not difficult to imagine that people from other places could have traded with both Palea and Lithos, thereby securing another reason for why the basket ended up there.

To summarize, if the author had discussed some specific evidence refuting the above possibilities, his claim could have been stronger. To evaluate the argument one needs to know many things conclusively such as whether people from either Palea or Lithos ever made any boat, whether there are any other way to cross the Brim River, or whether there was any other method of contact between the people of Palea and of Lithos. Thus, the argument makes an unsupportable claim using inadequate evidence. If the author provides the kind of specific information needed to determine the validity of the conclusion, the argument would become more logical.

Explanation of score 5

The given essay response is a great piece of work in its sharp ideas, clean arrangement of thoughts and strong hold on language.

The introduction concisely sums up the conclusion and explains crisply why the evidence to make the claim is insufficient.

The body paragraph contains all the major flaws, but not all the flaws (e.g. geological changes in the river). The flaws have been developed well. The response has clearly identified facets of the argument in a relevant manner according to the assigned task and developed them in a generally perceptive way [primary evidence is single basket, lack of evidence as evidence, etc]. Appropriate transitions have been used throughout the essay [the biggest flaw, furthermore, however, additionally, to summarize, etc]. The essay offers thoughtful and worthy considerations to strengthen the argument (the last paragraph).

The use of language is firm, displaying a proficient level of handling with the written language. The essay writer clearly has facility with the conventions of the written language and displays commendable knowledge of the vocabulary as well. The variety in good words – categorized, does not add up, critical, multitude, degenerated, refuting, etc.

The sentence variety is adequate – "The argument claims because ... anymore", "A single basket does not ... argument make", "That basket could have ... a multitude of ways!", However, what if Paleans ... aren't found?", "To evaluate the argument one needs to ... of Palea and of Lithos", etc.

All in all, strong and sharp work, deserving of score 5.

Sample Essay (Score 4)

The above argument states that Palean baskets cannot be thought of as uniquely Palean anymore. The author supports this claim by stating that one such "Palean" basket was found in Lithos, while as up to now such woven baskets with this distinctive pattern have only been found in the village of Palea. The author explains that the "Palean" basket found in Lithos has to be of Lithos because Lithos and Palea are separated by Brim River, which is very deep and broad and can be crossed only by boats. However, no Palean boats have been found yet. The argument may seem convincing but has numerous flaws, such as faulty assumptions and lack of evidence.

Firstly, the author states that the Brim River is very deep and broad, and could be crossed only by boat. Also that Palean boats haven't been found, and so there couldn't have been any exchange between Palea and Lithos. But, just stating this much does not prove that there was no connection between Palea and Lithos. For example, there is a distinct possibility that people of Lithos made boats using which they traded with the people of Palea. Also, Palean boats could be discovered at some point in the future, that is likely.

Secondly, the author provides no information about the histories of either Palea or Lithos, information gleaned from history, artifacts, ancient books, etc. This history is needed to evaluate certain possibilities. What if Palea and Lithos were one civilization but were later separated by the Brim River? Alternately, it could be that Paleans existed much before Lithos, and eventually left that area to settle in Lithos. These possibilities can weaken the conclusion. Thus, history of both Palea and Lithosis needed.

Finally, had the author addressed the various possibilities given above, the argument would have been more stronger and convincing. As if now, the argument is flawed.

Explanation of Score 4

The given essay response is adequate in its logic and structure but contains minor flaws in the language.

First and foremost, the introduction is too lengthy and detailed, almost replicating the entire argument piecemeal! Introductions should briefly summarize the argument in a general fashion. The details are meant for the body paragraphs.

The body paragraphs contain relevant points but lack discussion of some important flaws (single basket as primary evidence, lack of evidence being treated as evidence). However, the points have been developed in a satisfactory way. The writer presents the idea, explains its implications and discusses examples. Nevertheless, some extraneous points have been included. The entire second body paragraph seems to discuss flimsy points and stretched examples. It demonstrates lack of consistent thought process.

The conclusion is brief and unimaginative.

Transitions have been used throughout the essay but are completely trite ones [the above argument, firstly, also, but, secondly, finally, etc].

The use of language is basic, displaying a simple grasp on the written language. The knowledge of the vocabulary is meagre.

There is hardly any sentence variety, just a couple of "if" sentences. There are some errors - artifacts, more stronger, etc.

However, the overall reasoning is sound and structure clear, thus deserving a score 4.

Sample Essay (Score 2)

The author states that because a palean basket with distinctive weaving has been found in lithos, the baskets are not palean in origin, but they are lithos. The argument is convincing because it has furnished numerous evidences.

The argument gives good evidences to support its case. If a river is not crossed then there cannot be contact between two regions. So, clearly, therefore, lithos did not went to palea. No palea boats on lithos, so no crossing the river. So, even if upto now, palean baskets were in palea, one basket is in lithos. Also, no one can swim in deep and board river, or get drowned. It could be someone from another country came to palea and then went to lithos with the basket, but how possible? The basket in lithos is lithos's basket. Thus, the author is right to say that palean baskets are not uniquely palean but lithos baskets too.

Explanation of Score 2

The above essay is grossly off the mark in both logic and expression.

Logically, instead of finding the numerous possible flaws in the furnished evidence, the essay writer has spent time explaining the validity of the inadequate evidence! The organization of the essay is completely awry. Even though there seems to be some semblance of an introduction, the body and conclusion are not distinguishable from each other.

The use of language is extremely erroneous, to the point that reading and understanding it is nearly impossible. Some examples of language errors: lack of capitalization of proper nouns "Lithos" and "Palea", incorrect use of tenses "did not went"/ "drowned", incorrect punctuation (use of question mark instead of full stop) in the first sentence of the second paragraph.

All in all, the lack of discussing the flaws analytically, the lack of organized presentation and the flawed use of language leaves this essay response extremely shabby, and only deserving of a score 2.

6.2 Essay 2 (Monarch Books)

> The following is a recommendation from the Board of Directors of Monarch Books.
>
> "We recommend that Monarch Books open a café in its store. Monarch, having been in business at the same location for more than twenty years, has a large customer base because it is known for its wide selection of books on all subjects. Clearly, opening the café would attract more customers. Space could be made for the café by discontinuing the children's book section, which will probably become less popular given that the most recent national census indicated a significant decline in the percentage of the population under age ten. Opening a café will allow Monarch to attract more customers and better compete with Regal Books, which recently opened its own café."
>
> *Write a response in which you discuss what questions would need to be answered in order to decide whether the recommendation is likely to have the predicted result. Be sure to explain how the answers to these questions would help to evaluate the recommendation.*

Understand the argument

The given argument is a recommendation written by the Board of Directors of a book store called Monarch Books. The recommendation states that the Monarch should open a cafe within the store. Multiple reasons have been cited for this recommendation. Primary reason seems to be that the Board of Directors of Monarch is wary of Regal Books and wishes to maintain its position in the market. Regal Books has recently opened a cafe. Additional support has been given about why opening a cafe is beneficial. The Board explains in the recommendation that since Monarch has been at the same location for more than twenty years, the store has a big customer base, and is well-known among the public for its wide-selection of books on every topic. The space for the cafe can be made by clearing out the part in which children's books are kept. According to the Board, clearing out the children's books will not have a negative impact because the latest census states that there's a significant decline in the percentage of population that is under ten years of age.

Recommendation/Conclusion: Opening a café will allow Monarch to attract more customers and better compete with Regal Books.

Faulty assumptions

- Removing children's section will not damage reputation of stocking wide variety of books

- The latest census is recent, and not very old

- The significant decline in the percentage of the population under age ten will equal a significant decline in numbers of customers for children's books too

- Children's books don't account for a substantial part of current sales

- Opening a cafe will not detract from the sales of the bookstore itself

Missing evidence

- Details about the census – when was it conducted, how much is the actual expected percentage of children under ten years, what is the number of children under ten years

- Information about impact on reputation of the store, if it removes an entire section of children's books

- How much of the current sales do children's books account for?

- Information about whether book sales will get impacted if a cafe is opened

- Details of the costs of scrapping the children's section and setting up a cafe and about how long it will take to recover the investment

Counter-examples

- What if the number of children under ten years of age is still significant?

- What if a large portion of Monarch Books' sales is made up by sales of children's books?

- What if the reputation of Monarch is considerably damaged by removing an entire section, enough to impact its sales?

- What if people start coming to Monarch for its cafes and not its books?

- What if the census is more than 6-7 years old and therefore does not have updated statistics on current population under ten years old?

Once you have pinned down at least a couple of flaws and their relevant missing evidence, as well as created a few counter-examples to weaken the argument's conclusion, start writing the essay. New points may occur to you as you construct your essay, but incorporate them into your essay only if they blend in with your analysis so far. Resist the urge to include too many points; overkill spoils a sharp essay. However, important points related to the primary structure of the argument must always be included in the essay.

Sample Essay (Score 6)

The Board of Directors of Monarch Books recommends setting up a cafe within the bookstore, chiefly because Regal Books, Monarch's competitor, has recently done so. The Board has corroborated its recommendation with numerous tokens to serve as testimony to the soundness of the plan. Regrettably, the brilliant suggestion has been tarnished by lack of integral data that would create the entire picture needed to evaluate this decision.

The biggest flaw with the argument lies in its failure to provide holistic pieces of evidence. Each of the so-called premises meant to support the Board's recommendation lacks indispensable aspects of information. Even though the Board does not provide a concrete reason to setup a cafe, the idea of a cosy cafe within a bookstore is not unattractive, the pairing seems natural. However, a cafe simply to ape Regal's move seems illogical. Starting with the census as a basis for removing children's section to make place for the cafe, the Board has not discussed actual numbers, but merely stated that a significant decline in percentage of children under ten years of age is predicted. However, actual numbers can paint a different picture. Further, the age of the census will determine its relevance. A presumably old census may not provide accurate details about how many under ten year olds are around! Assuming everything is according to the Board's expectation and the percentage and number of children under ten has indeed declined, that decline would apply as a national average, but not necessarily in every city at the same percentage;. So, the area in which Monarch has its store could still house a substantial number of children, thus putting the move to remove the children's section under a shadow. Additionally, the Board acknowledges that Monarch has built up, over a period of twenty years, a reputation for stocking books on all subjects. It is believed that reputation and goodwill generate business even without any marketing. Wouldn't removing an entire line of books hurt that very reputation? Offending the patrons of the bookstore, simply to put in a cafe does not seem worth the probable benefits, as they may be. Nevertheless, if numbers demonstrate that a cafe is a lucrative move, the Board should first ascertain the sales made up by children's books, to ensure that a precipitate move does not endanger extant profits.

Notwithstanding the flaws in the furnished evidence, the idea of a cafe in a bookstore bears further pursuing. What must be determined is whether the customers like the notion of a cafe, what sort of cafe - fancy or informal - would they prefer, and whether a cafe will detract the customers from the bookstore itself. Proper data collection and feasibility planning can turn this enticing concept into fruitful reality.

To conclude, the recommendation by the Board of Directions contains a gem of an idea swaddled by deficient data. Proper attention can yield a brilliant business plan. All the same, the recommendation fails to do a convincing job in its current state.

Explanation of score 6

The given essay response contains brilliant and insightful logic, skilled and thoughtful organization and compelling use of language.

The introduction sums up the conclusion in a pithy way and crisply mentions why the evidence to make the claim is insufficient.

The body paragraph clearly makes the point that the biggest problem is that every piece of evidence is insufficient by itself and does not add up to its claim. The writer then starts by stating that while the reason for a cafe is not given, the idea of a cafe contains promise. The essay further explains how each piece of evidence is inadequate. Proper substantiation is given whenever needed. Each of the points has been developed thoroughly. The second body paragraph shows perception on the part of the writer because it contains the specific questions that must be answered to evaluate the idea. This paragraph demonstrates that the essay writer was aware of the specific question asked about the given argument.

The conclusion is sharp and sums up the critique well, by explaining why the argument is invalid. The ideas display incisive logically (cafe per se is a good idea, details before removing children's section, the possibility that the census is misleading) and the development is gradual and complex. There are no holes in the thought process.
The precise use of transition words throughout the essay demonstrates thoughtful writing skill [the biggest flaw, even though, however, starting with, further, assuming everything, thus, additionally, nevertheless, notwithstanding, etc].

The use of language is excellent, displaying a superb level of dexterity with the written language. The essay writer clearly has an adept grip on the conventions of the written language and displays impressive facility with the vocabulary as well.

The variety in precise words – corroborated, tokens, testimony, soundness, regrettably, tarnished, integral, holistic, indispensable, concrete, etc.

The sentence variety is astonishing for a work created under time constraints – various "if" clauses, many rhetorical questions, inverted sentences, exclamatory sentences, etc.

All in all, superb work, deserving of score 6.

Sample Essay (Score 5)

The given argument deals with Monarch Books, which is well-known for carrying books on all sections. The Board of Directors of Monarch advises that a cafe should be opened in the store, the way Monarch's competitor Regal Books has done. The Board has furnished some evidence towards the case made. While the plan has some logic to it, it suffers from a lack of important information, leading to hasty assumptions.

The primary flaw in the argument is that the recommendation of making a cafe begs the question why. Even if we assume that the cafe should be made to not be out-competed by Regal Books and also to progress, complete data is not given to make this decision in an informed manner. The argument states that children's section should be cleared out based on the latest census, albeit without information about the relevance of the census, about number of children in the population, about how many sales of Monarch are linked to children's section, about the cost of setting up a cafe. Each of these missing pieces of information can completely skew the outcome of setting up a cafe. If the reputation of Monarch Books is that it stocks books of all varieties, clearing out an entire section may just put people off Monarch even if there are very few customers who buy children's books, and such is the impact of brand image! Also, relying on a census makes sense only if it's a recent one, say conducted in the past couple of years or so. However, since, a census is usually done once in a decade, the census used may very well be nine years old, after which many children may have been born who are under ten and potential customers of Monarch. Further, even if the census were recent, a significant percentage decline does not have to impact the numbers considerably. The number of under the age of ten children may very well favor retaining the children's section. Finally, no details about the financial impact of setting up a cafe have been provided in the recommendation.

The recommendation cannot be truly evaluated in a logical way until these key pieces of information that can influence the result greatly are supplied. If the Board of Directors had taken all the above factors into consideration in making the recommendation, the argument would have survived the critique better than it has.

Explanation of score 5

The given essay response is strong, well-written with minimum errors in the language. The introduction is crisp and explains the overall situation in the argument well, but could have been better-knit with connectors showing the correct cause- and-effect relationship of the recommendation and its premises.

The body paragraph unfolds and presents all its points well with clean and precise organization. The body starts by explaining that no actual reason for the entire recommendation has been given in a clear way and whatever has been given lacks important aspects. The ideas have been well-supported with proper description and credible examples. However, some awkwardness in discussion is present, example "The argument states that children's section ... the cost of setting up a cafe".

Sentence variety is good but not great, with most sentences following complex styles. However, commendable vocabulary saves the writing quite a lot (begs the question, out-competed, albeit, furnished, skew, etc). Also, different connectors in the body improve the readability immensely (even if, and such, only if, say, until, etc) The conclusion is written in a brilliant flourish, adding sharp expression to the overall essay and raising the level of the essay.

All in all, slightly inconsistent in language but sharp in logic and thus, deserving of a score 5.

Sample Essay (Score 4)

Monarch Books suggests that it should open a cafe inside its store. , Regal Books is Monarch's competitor and it has also opened a cafe inside its store. Further, Monarch wishes to remove the children's section from the store to make place for the cafe because the census dictates that the percentage of population under age ten has declined significantly. Although the recommendation sounds logical, many pieces of key evidence are missing to make this judgment.

To begin with, the author provides no information about the census at all. The census could be very old or very new, and that would affect its significance. If it is old, things may have changed. Further, the author does not state what it would cost to make a cafe and remove the children's section and whether such plans will be overall profitable. Also, the author does not explain what impact the move will have on the image of Monarch Books. Regular customers of Monarch might find removing children's section unacceptable. Bad publicity can affect any business, especially a company that has been around for 20 years has to keep up with high expectations. It is also possible that building a cafe might affect the bookstore, if people start coming for the cafe rather than the books itself.

To conclude, if Monarch Books wants to keep its customers from shifting to Regal Books, maybe it should conduct a survey of customers from both and check what specifically the customers would like. Just copying Regal will not differentiate Monarch. Also, relying on merely census records is not a wise move. Detailed information is needed. Further, before taking any hasty steps, proper evaluation of the implications of each step must be analyzed. Had the author noted all these alternatives, the argument would have been stronger than it is now.

Explanation of Score 4

The given essay response is satisfactory as far as logic and organization are concerned but contains inconsistency in both.

Primarily, the introduction is too detailed and bulky, almost repeating the entire argument. Introductions are meant to succinctly sum up the argument in a general manner and not to provide meaty details. The details are meant for the body paragraphs.

The body paragraphs contain relevant points but lack discussion of some important flaws (percentages do not reveal numbers, distribution of children over regions, etc.). However, the points have been presented in an adequate way. The writer presents the points, discusses their implications and at times provides examples. However, the response demonstrates lack of consistent thought process. For example, the point about conducting a survey in the concluding paragraph is strong enough to be added into the main body paragraph and developed further. However, it's been treated as a subsidiary point, not worth mentioning until the very end. On the other hand, a relatively minor point about image has been stretched thin in the main body paragraph, diluting the focus of the logic.

The conclusion redeems the essay by its important logical point. Nevertheless, the conclusion is not the place to make new points. It is only meant to sum up the points and provide a suitable end. Connectors have been used but are completely unimaginative ones [the above argument, to begin with, to conclude, etc.].

The use of language is basic, displaying a simple grasp on the written language. The knowledge of the vocabulary is meagre with a few surprisingly good words – dictates, key evidence, differentiate, relying, merely, etc.

There is hardly any sentence variety, just a couple of "if" sentences. Also, shuttling between the use of "Monarch Books" and "the author" is disconcerting.

Notwithstanding the inconsistency, the overall reasoning is sound and structure clear, thus deserving a score 4.

Sample Essay (Score 2)

The Board of Directors of Monarch is saying that cafe will be opened in the bookstore. Regal Books has did the same recently. To make decision about this, evidence is needed but only partly been given. The argument is good but needs more details to make it more better.

Firstly, the recommendation did not discuss how the census applied to customers of Monarch books? It not always that only childrens buys childrens books. Some comics are bought by old people and adults also. How much that will affect the sales and profit? Also, how a cafe can be successful inside a bookstore? Secondly, what if regals cafee and book cheapest than monarch? More costly prices can effect customers more then cafe. More detail should be about why regal got cafe and its effect on monarch. Also, how far regal is from monarch?

In summassion, boards needs to discuss why cafe to be opened, how census works, who buy childrens books and how far regal and monarch. No details makes argument more weakened.

Explanation of Score 2

The above essay is terrible in its logic and incomprehensible in its expression. The points being made have been completely obscured by the atrocious use of language. However, some semblance of understanding leads one to believe that a couple of important points have been discussed, (relevance of the census, need of the cafe), however illegibly.

The examples seem beyond absurd and are downright bizarre! [the comics for adults]. The use of written communication leaves very much to be desired. Grammar is completely missing, and some words have been victimized [buyed, childrens, summassion].

However, some appearance of logic and painful but present use of transitions earns this essay response the scant score of 2.

6.3 Essay 3 (Investment advice)

> The following appeared in a letter from a firm providing investment advice to a client.
>
> "Homes in the northeastern United States, where winters are typically cold, have traditionally used oil as their major fuel for heating. Last year that region experienced twenty days with below-average temperatures, and local weather forecasters throughout the region predict that this weather pattern will continue for several more years. Furthermore, many new homes have been built in this region during the past year. Because of these developments, we predict an increased demand for heating oil and recommend investment in Consolidated Industries, one of whose major business operations is the retail sale of home heating oil."
>
> *Write a response in which you discuss what specific evidence is needed to evaluate the argument and explain how the evidence would weaken or strengthen the argument.*

Understand the argument

The argument is written by a firm that is providing investment advice to a client. The firm's advice is that its client should invest in Consolidated Industries, which is involved in retail sales of home heating oil. The firm predicts that there will be an increased demand for heating oil, as the basis for recommending investment in Consolidated Industries. The firm makes the prediction on the basis of the facts that homes in NE USA have traditionally used oil to heat their homes. The firm also provides weather details of last year that the region had twenty days below-average temperature and this trend is expected to continue for many years. Another piece supporting the prediction of increased demand for heating oil is that many new homes have been built in this region during the past year, implying more consumption of oil and in turn good business prospects for Consolidated Industries, as well as for anyone who invests in Consolidated Industries.

Recommendation/Conclusion: Invest in Consolidated Industries.

Faulty assumptions

- The homes still use heating oil to warm the house

- The extra oil used on those 20 days with below average temperatures will not be compensated by reduced consumption of oil in reasonably comfortable days?

- New homes will also continue to use the traditional method of heating homes using oil

- Consolidated Industries meets the majority of the demand of home heating oil in that region; no other company selling home heating oil is worth investing in

Missing evidence

· Details about the heating methods used by the new homes built in the area, as well as by the current methods used by the existing homes

· Details about home heating oil used over the past years, especially the extra oil use due to 20 days with below average temperatures

· About the average temperature and of number of days reasonably comfortable days and its expected trend in the next few years

· Details about the market share of Consolidated Industries and a competition analysis of the market

Counter-examples

· What if the homes have shifted to another method of heating the house?

· What if lot of days of the last year had above average temperatures, leading to reduced used of oil?

· What if companies other than Consolidated Industries have a better share of the market and better profit margins than does Consolidated Industries?

Once you have pinned down at least a couple of flaws and their relevant missing evidence, as well as created a few counter-examples to weaken the argument's conclusion, start writing the essay. New points may occur to you as you construct your essay, but incorporate them into your essay only if they blend in with your analysis so far. Resist the urge to include too many points; overkill spoils a sharp essay. However, important points related to the primary structure of the argument must always be included in the essay.

Essay

In the given argument, a firm advises a client to invest in Consolidated Industries which sells heating oil meant for homes. This recommendation is based on the premise that heating oil demand is likely to go up given the rise in number of homes constructed and a drop in average temperatures, necessitating the use of home heating oil. The argument sounds reasonable but only initially and a detailed analysis reveals multiple flawed assumptions, rendering the investment advice unsound.

To begin with, the firm states that homes in north-eastern United States traditionally use heating oil, assuming that this convention continues unchanged. However, the firm seems to have made no move to confirm that the homes in north-eastern United States would not have changed with the times and shifted to newer technology not directly dependent on home heating oil, say, perhaps radiant heating or electric resistance heating systems, neither of which require home heating oil. Determining this fact is a basic necessity and failure to do so reeks of thoughtless planning on the firm's part.

Another flawed assumption the firm makes concerns the meteorological trivia of 20 days with below average temperatures, relegated as trivia in the absence of information about days with above average temperatures. Assuming that the homes still do use home heating oil, if, out of 365 days of the year, even 30 to 40 days were reasonably comfortable days, the reduced use of home heating oil on those days would offset the increased use of the oil on the 20 days with below average temperatures. However, the firm seems to have missed noticing the remaining 345 days in discussing the 20 days with below average temperatures.

Yet another oversight on the firm's part is lack of market information when it recommends investment in Consolidated Industries. All that the firm deems fit to mention is that Consolidated Industries are involved in the sale of home heating oil. What about the market share of Consolidated Industries and what are its profit margins? Are the competitors of Consolidated Industries better investment options? These unanswered questions present the client with no worthy choices.

To conclude, what the firm needs is to reassess its advice by substantiating its assumptions with information on heating methods used by the homes in north-eastern United States, on the temperatures on the remaining 345 days, and on detailed analysis of the home heating oil market as well as on Consolidated Industries. Lack of consideration in all these aspects leaves the investment advice thoroughly unconvincing.

6.4   Essay 4 (Balmer Island)

> The following appeared in a letter to the editor of the Balmer Island Gazette.
>
> "On Balmer Island, where mopeds serve as a popular form of transportation, the population increases to 100,000 during the summer months. To reduce the number of accidents involving mopeds and pedestrians, the town council of Balmer Island should limit the number of mopeds rented by the island's moped rental companies from 50 per day to 25 per day during the summer season. By limiting the number of rentals, the town council will attain the 50 percent annual reduction in moped accidents that was achieved last year on the neighboring island of Seaville, when Seaville's town council enforced similar limits on moped rentals."
>
> *Write a response in which you discuss what questions would need to be answered in order to decide whether the recommendation is likely to have the predicted result. Be sure to explain how the answers to these questions would help to evaluate the recommendation.*

Understand the argument

A letter has been written to the editor of the Balmer Island Gazette. The writer recommends restricting the number of moped rentals from 50 to 25 per day during the summer season on Balmer Island (where mopeds are favored). The writer recommends so because he believes that this reduction will achieve a 50% reduction in moped accidents. To support his claims, he presents Seaville, which apparently imposed similar restrictions and got 50% reduction in moped accidents. The summer season seems to be the problem because during summer season, the population of Balmer increases to 100,000.

Conclusion: Restrict the number of moped rentals from 50 to 25 per day during the summer season on Balmer Island to achieve a 50% reduction in moped accidents.

Faulty assumptions

- Restricting the number of mopeds will not affect businesses/tourism and will reduce the number of moped accidents

- No other way of reducing moped accidents; the number of moped accidents are directly proportional to number of mopeds

- Seaville is exactly identical to Balmer Island

Missing evidence

- Analysis of why moped accidents happen and any prevention methods other than restricting rentals

- Information about impact of restricting the number of moped rentals on tourism, on public transport, etc

- Specifics and proof about how exactly Seaville is similar to Balmer Island with respect to moped accidents and its reduction, among other things

Counter-examples

- What if the number of moped accidents remains the same even during the summer months, even after restricting the number of moped rentals?

- What if moped accidents are caused because of lack of awareness of traffic rules rather than by number of mopeds itself?

- What if some measures like widening the roads, or smoothening them can reduce the moped accidents drastically without having to restrict the number of mopeds?

Once you have pinned down at least a couple of flaws and their relevant missing evidence, as well as created a few counter-examples to weaken the argument's conclusion, start writing the essay. New points may occur to you as you construct your essay, but incorporate them into your essay only if they blend in with your analysis so far. Resist the urge to include too many points; overkill spoils a sharp essay. However, important points related to the primary structure of the argument must always be included in the essay.

Essay

In a letter to the editor of the Balmer Gazette, a writer claims that restricting the number of mopeds being rented during the summer months when population increases, the number of moped accidents can be cut by half. Various premises have been provided to support this claim. Unfortunately, multiple necessary questions have been left unanswered posed by this claim, making it unlikely that the proposed action will have its intended effect.

The primary flaw in the claim is that implication that the number of mopeds is directly proportional to the number of moped accidents. To carry this logic further, it would make sense to even suggest that mopeds should be banned altogether to prevent moped accidents! No reason for restricting the number of mopeds has been provided except that Seaville did the same and achieved a commensurate reduction in moped accidents. It is far more likely that the moped accidents are caused by lack of awareness of traffic rules, possibly bumpy roads, absence of traffic managements among other factors. While restricting mopeds may reduce the moped accidents, the cause may remain unaddressed and therefore, the problem will remain unresolved. As for Seaville's move, the writer has possibly been as hasty with this reference, as he has been with others, and not provided exact details as to Seaville's situation and the methods employed by it. What if Seaville reduced the number of moped accidents by introducing a host of measures, of which one was restricting the number of mopeds? There is also the likelihood that Seaville faced repercussions of restricting the number of mopeds in the form of protests from moped rental businesses, negative response from tourists, outrage from residents, etc. In absence of contextual details, analyzing this example in vacuum seems fraught with risk.

In conclusion, the writer needs to revisit the argument and substantiate his premises and claims with appropriate data, specifically, information about the extent of population is increase in the summer, details about number of moped accidents during other months compared to that in the summer, information about impact of restricting the number of moped rentals and specifics about Seaville's comparability to Balmer Island with respect to moped accidents and its reduction, among other things. Most of all, the writer's claim would benefit from a detailed analysis of why moped accidents happen on Balmer Island and whether there are any prevention methods other than restricting rentals of mopeds. Only after such information is made available, can the argument be considered justified and evaluated further. Nevertheless, the claim currently is far from convincing.

6.5 Essay 5 (Mentian advertising executives)

> The following appeared as part of an article in a business magazine.
>
> "A recent study rating 300 male and female Mentian advertising executives according to the average number of hours they sleep per night showed an association between the amount of sleep the executives need and the success of their firms. Of the advertising firms studied, those whose executives reported needing no more than 6 hours of sleep per night had higher profit margins and faster growth. These results suggest that if a business wants to prosper, it should hire only people who need less than 6 hours of sleep per night."
>
> *Write a response in which you examine the stated and/or unstated assumptions of the argument. Be sure to explain how the argument depends on these assumptions and what the implications are for the argument if the assumptions prove unwarranted.*

Understand the argument

In a business magazine, a writer claims that a business should hire only those people who need less than 6 hours of sleep per night, if the business wants to prosper. The writer makes this claim based on a recent study of 300 male and female Mentian advertising executives. This study found that executives who need less than 6 hours of sleep per night had higher profit margins and faster growth. So, the writer concludes that the number of hours of sleep needed per night by an executive is linked to that executive's profit margins and growth, specifically that executives who need 6 hours or less sleep per night have higher profit margins and faster growth.

Claim: If a business wants to prosper, it should hire only those people who need less than 6 hours of sleep per night.

Faulty assumptions

- These 300 Mentian advertising executives are representative of employees of any business vertical in general.

- Other factors responsible for higher profit margins and faster growth in those executives except their sleep patterns are insignificant.

- All businesses are similar to advertising firms

Missing evidence

- Exact details of the people surveyed to check whether the advertising executives represent employees of any business vertical in general

- Proof about how all businesses are similar to advertising firms and will have same results by hiring executives who need 6 hours or less sleep

- Details about other factors that may be responsible for higher profit margins and faster growth in those executives other than their sleep patterns

Counter-examples

- What if the executives represent only a certain type of group among people and not all the employees of any business vertical in general?

- What if only advertising firms have specific needs that make certain types of executives fare better, but the firms are different from other types of firms?

- What if the more successful executives are better in some other aspects such as better education or more experience, which is directly responsible for their success rather than their sleep patterns?

Once you have pinned down at least a couple of flaws and their relevant missing evidence, as well as created a few counter-examples to weaken the argument's conclusion, start writing the essay. New points may occur to you as you construct your essay, but incorporate them into your essay only if they blend in with your analysis so far. Resist the urge to include too many points; overkill spoils a sharp essay. However, important points related to the primary structure of the argument must always be included in the essay.

Essay

In a business magazine, a writer asserts that, in order to be successful, businesses should hire only those people who need 6 hours or less sleep. The writer backs his assertion up by citing a recent study. The argument is completely irresponsible as it relies on multiple flawed assumptions and provides only partial evidence.

To begin with, the argument uses a study on only 300 advertising executives to make a claim that would apply to all executives of all companies of any business vertical. Demonstrating utter carelessness, the writer does not specify at all how a study on advertising executives can be extrapolated to all business executives, let alone prove that these 300 advertising executives are representative of advertising executives! If these assumptions are taken apart and challenged, the whole claim would crumble! Without concrete evidence, it is impossible to believe that merely 300 Mentian advertising executives represent all advertising executives, or generally all executives. A small slice of advertising business is most likely what the survey contains, and thereby applying it to anything more than just that slice of advertising business is unacceptable.

Furthermore, even if we are to turn a blind eye to the validity of the survey applying to all businesses, that precious little has been mentioned about these 300 Mentian advertising executives is another glaring oversight. The writer finds that certain advertising executives are more successful than others and also that the same executives sleep no more than 6 hours and promptly assumes that these two aspects are related, without sparing a single thought to other characteristics of those successful executives that makes them successful. A mere positive correlation between two factors does not a cause-and-effect relationship make! In absence of data about the education, work experience, personal characteristics of those surveyed executives, it is impossible to even begin to evaluate what specifically makes them successful. To attempt to do so leads to such absurd connections as the type shown in the argument by the writer.

In conclusion, the argument suffers from flawed assumptions that can be resolved only if the writer provides sufficient evidence, specifically, details of the people surveyed to ascertain whether the advertising executives are representative, as well as details about other aspects that may be responsible for higher profit margins and faster growth in those executives other than their sleep patterns, and proof about how all businesses are similar to advertising firms and will achieve the same results by hiring executives who need 6 hours or less sleep. In its current state, the claim stands thoroughly vulnerable to criticism and absolutely unconvincing.

6.6   Essay 6 (Radio station WCQP)

> Two years ago, radio station WCQP in Rockville decided to increase the number of call-in advice programs that it broadcast; since that time, its share of the radio audience in the Rockville listening area has increased significantly. Given WCQP's recent success with call-in advice programming, and citing a nationwide survey indicating that many radio listeners are quite interested in such programs, the station manager of KICK in Medway recommends that KICK include more call-in advice programs in an attempt to gain a larger audience share in its listening area.
>
> *Write a response in which you discuss what questions would need to be answered in order to decide whether the recommendation and the argument on which it is based are reasonable. Be sure to explain how the answers to these questions would help to evaluate the recommendation.*

Understand the argument

In the above argument, a station manager of a radio station, KICK, in the city Medway states that KICK, to get larger audience, should add more programs that have call-in advice. This recommendation is based on success from a similar move made by radio station WCQP in Rockville. Also, the station manager of KICK cites a national survey that found that more listeners preferred call-in advice programs.

Faulty assumptions

- WCQP and KICK are exactly comparable in all respects
- The national survey would necessarily apply to Medway
- Other measures to gain larger audience are not worthy

Missing evidence

- Details about how WCQP is comparable to KICK
- Whether the statistics of the national survey apply in the same proportion to Medway too
- Any other things KICK can do to gain larger audience, such as a survey conducted on radio listeners

Counter-examples

- What if WCQP and KICK cater to completely different audiences?
- What if Medway's population is different from the national average?

- What if KICK can improve other things such as quality of music, variety, etc to gain larger audience?

- What if KICK has a niche yet loyal audience base that is due to the programs other than call-in advice programs?

Essay

In the city of Medway, the station manager of a radio station known as KICK recommends including certain type of programs, based on another station's success in including the same and a national survey showing listeners' preference for those types of programs. The argument does contain a good idea, but, unfortunately, the idea lacks proper substantiation and has been clouded over by faulty assumptions.

To begin with, the station manager, in recommending WCQP's actions to KICK, completely disregards whether these two stations are even comparable. Just because both are radio stations does not imply that both necessarily cater to similar audiences: one could be rock-music station while the other could air classical symphonies! To merely assume that KICK would do well with a certain program because another radio station has is meaningless unless it is made clear that both WCQP is similar to KICK, in most respects. To remedy this flaw, the station manager should do an exhaustive analysis of the two radio stations and establish that these two fall in the same categories of radio stations and cater to audiences similar in type and demographics.

Furthermore, the author cites a national survey that found that listeners prefer call-in advice programs. National figures indicate an overall national preference that does not necessarily apply to every city. For example, if a survey states that the children make up 25% of the nation's population, not every city or state would necessarily have 25% of children in its population, some cities may have significantly more than 25% of children, while others may have significantly below, bringing the national average to 25%. Likewise for a national survey, indicating listeners preference of call-in advice programs. It does not have to apply to Medway. The station manager should have ascertained whether the listeners of KICK prefer call-in advice programs as well.

In conclusion, call-in advice programs sound like an interesting and possibly profitable addition to a radio station's repertoire. However, hastily implementing such additions without determining the preferences of the listeners of the radio station, the decision is fraught with risk. Therefore, the given argument is rendered unsound and unconvincing.

6.7   Essay 7 (Arctic deer)

> Arctic deer live on islands in Canada's arctic regions. They search for food by moving over ice from island to island during the course of the year. Their habitat is limited to areas warm enough to sustain the plants on which they feed and cold enough, at least some of the year, for the ice to cover the sea separating the islands, allowing the deer to travel over it. Unfortunately, according to reports from local hunters, the deer populations are declining. Since these reports coincide with recent global warming trends that have caused the sea ice to melt, we can conclude that the purported decline in deer populations is the result of the deer's being unable to follow their age-old migration patterns across the frozen sea.
>
> *Write a response in which you discuss what specific evidence is needed to evaluate the argument and explain how the evidence would weaken or strengthen the argument.*

Understand the argument

In the argument, the author provides information about Arctic deer that live in arctic regions of Canada, on islands. Unfortunately, this deer population is declining. The author feels that the deer population is declining because of general reports of global warming that typically leads to melted sea ice. The deer population would be very much affected by melted sea ice because the deer need frozen sea ice at least part of the year to migrate to other islands to look for food by traveling over the frozen sea. However, the deer also need a certain amount of warmth in the areas they live, because without warmth the plants that the deer feed on would not grow.

Claim: Deer population living on islands in Canada's arctic regions is declining due to recent global warming trends.

Faulty assumptions

- No other factor is significantly causing the deer population to decline
- Global warming has necessarily prevented the sea around islands in Canada's arctic regions from freezing
- No other factor is responsible for preventing the sea around islands in Canada's arctic regions from freezing

Missing evidence

- Specific details about whether the sea around islands in Canada's arctic regions has become frozen or remained fluid
- Details about other factors that may have negative effects on the deer population
- About other factors that may affect the freezing of the sea around islands in Canada's arctic regions

Counter-examples

- What if the sea around islands in Canada's arctic regions has become frozen?

- What if the deer population has gone down because of excessive hunting?

- What if global warming has changed the vegetation pattern in islands in Canada's arctic regions, leaving very little food for the deer population?

- What if some exploration project or offshore drilling is affecting the freezing cycles of the sea around islands in Canada's arctic regions?

Essay

In the given argument, the author claims that recent global warming trends are directly responsible for the declining deer population in Canada's arctic regions. To substantiate his claims, the author provides numerous premises about the needs of the deer. Given the recent surfeit of negative effects quite probably directly attributable to global warming, this claim may have some germ of truth in it. However, lack of supporting evidence and the dependence on faulty assumptions has left the argument unsound.

To begin with, the author seems to have just stated that a certain alarming event directly coincides with recent global warming trends, without explaining whether global warming has yet affected the sea around islands in Canada's arctic regions has become frozen. While such an inference may have been implied, not explicitly stating that the sea around islands in Canada's arctic regions has become frozen leaves the claim at least a bit dubious. Merely stating that two events have positive correlation does not make those two events necessarily cause and effect. However, it is quite believable that global warming has probably kept the sea around islands in Canada's arctic regions from becoming frozen. Assuming just so, the author still misses the mark by not discussing the various other factors that may have had a significant impact on the deer population. What if deer hunting has considerably increased in these regions reducing the number of deer? Alternatively, it is quite likely that global warming has altered the food quantities available to the deer population, impacting their numbers. Likewise, some projects in arctic regions, such as offshore drilling or arctic exploration, may pose a threat to the flora and fauna of the region, including the deer population. Lacking evidence on these possible factors that could have caused the deer population to decline, the argument is vulnerable to criticism.

In conclusion, the argument is poorly constructed in haste. Decline in native fauna, such as deer population living on the islands in Canada's arctic regions, is a complex event, affected by multiple issues, issues like natural predators, food availability, competition for survival, etc. A thorough analysis of the issue needs to be done to pin down the problem and its various causative agents. Only after such an exhaustive investigation can available solutions be measured and implemented. Simply blaming the hot topic in the news for the event, true as it may have been, without substantiating the claims with requisite proof, makes the argument unconvincing.

6.8   Essay 8 (Happy Pancake House restaurants)

> *The following memorandum is from the business manager of Happy Pancake House restaurants.*
>
> "Recently, butter has been replaced by margarine in Happy Pancake House restaurants throughout the southwestern United States. This change, however, has had little impact on our customers. In fact, only about 2 percent of customers have complained, indicating that an average of 98 people out of 100 are happy with the change. Furthermore, many servers have reported that a number of customers who ask for butter do not complain when they are given margarine instead. Clearly, either these customers do not distinguish butter from margarine or they use the term 'butter' to refer to either butter or margarine."
>
> *Write a response in which you discuss one or more alternative explanations that could rival the proposed explanation and explain how your explanation(s) can plausibly account for the facts presented in the argument.*

Understand the argument

A business manager of Happy Pancake House restaurants has issued a memo claiming that serving margarine instead of butter has had no impact on the customers. The manager thinks so because he states that only 2% of customers complained about this change. Thus, the manager infers that the other 98% are satisfied with the change and only 2% are unhappy. He further believes that the customers cannot tell the difference between butter and margarine or the customers think that the term "butter" includes both butter and margarine.

Claim: Serving margarine instead of butter has had no impact on the customers at Happy Pancake House restaurants.

Faulty assumptions

- Only 2% complained means only 2% unhappy

- The other 98% haven't complained means they cannot distinguish between butter and margarine or think margarine is included under the term "butter"

- Replacing butter with margarine will not significantly affect the business

Missing evidence

- Information about whether business has dropped after replacing butter with margarine

- More details about the customers' response, especially of the regular ones, details such as polls or surveys about whether the customers are okay with replacing butter with margarine

- Particulars about whether regular patrons of the restaurants have reduced in number

Counter-examples

- What if only the most upset customers complained and many more are upset but not bothered about complaining?

- What if the regular patrons of Happy Pancake House restaurants have switched to some other restaurants and the 98% are mostly made up of new customers who never knew that the restaurant served butter?

- What if the customers are giving negative reviews to Happy Pancake House restaurants elsewhere eve if they don't complain to the restaurant itself?

Essay

A business manager claims that substituting margarine with butter has not impacted customers at Happy Pancake House restaurants. The manager bases his claims on the fact that only two percent of customers have complained about this change. The memo by the manager could have been more convincing had certain assumptions been substantiated with proper evidence.

The primary flaw in the argument is the misconception of the manager that 98 percent of customers are happy, if only 2 percent have complained. The business manager assumes that every customer who has problems with any particular change that has been implemented will complain. However, not all disgruntled customers do. Typically, only the ones most annoyed by the changes end up formally complaining. Most customers, even if unhappy at the change from butter to margarine, would simply take note of the unhappy instance and probably pass that on to friends and family. In such a scenario, the customers would either stop patronizing the restaurant altogether or give the restaurant a few more chances before switching to some other, more amenable eatery. Thus, the manager misses a step in assuming that the 2 percent of complainants represent all those who are unhappy. The number is quite possibly much higher. Without knowing the actual proportion of those who are unhappy with the change, judging whether replacing butter with margarine has affected the business negatively is difficult. For all we know, many regular customers may have already switched to some other eatery that actually serves butter.

Apart from the mistaken assumption about the percent of customers unhappy with the change is the conspicuous lack of information about the motivations for this entire exercise. Replacing butter with margarine can actually be a good move from both the customers' and the restaurant's point of view. Margarine is considered a healthy variant of butter and used by many health conscious people in lieu of butter. Margarine is also cheaper than butter. Ergo, this move can create a win-win situation, but only if executed correctly. If a poll of customers is taken, the restaurant can get details about the preferences of the customers and accordingly offer a healthier variant to those who want it. In this manner, the customers would not feel as though something has been thrust upon them without their prior consent and the restaurant gets a chance to become more customer-savvy, possibly even attract more customers. Thus, implementing this change should have been done with proper data, which is lacking in the given memo.

To conclude, if the business manager had discussed why this change was put into effect, what the customers feel about this change and what the benefit of this change is, the memo would have been stronger. As it stands, the memo seems vulnerable on account of its faulty assumptions and lack of evidence.

6.9   Essay 9 (Quiot Manufacturing)

The following appeared in a memo from a vice president of Quiot Manufacturing.

"During the past year, Quiot Manufacturing had 30 percent more on-the-job accidents than at the nearby Panoply Industries plant, where the work shifts are one hour shorter than ours. Experts say that significant contributing factors in many on-the-job accidents are fatigue and sleep deprivation among workers. Therefore, to reduce the number of on-the-job accidents at Quiot and thereby increase productivity, we should shorten each of our three work shifts by one hour so that employees will get adequate amounts of sleep."

Write a response in which you examine the stated and/or unstated assumptions of the argument. Be sure to explain how the argument depends on these assumptions and what the implications are for the argument if the assumptions prove unwarranted.

Understand the argument

The VP of a company called Quiot Manufacturing suggests that the company should reduce each of its work hour shifts by one hour to allow them to sleep more. This is suggested as a primary solution to the issue that the company has had 30% more on-the-job accidents than Panoply Industries. To support this suggestion the VP provides 2 premises ? 1) that another company, Panoply Industries, reduced its work-hour shifts and has had fewer on-the-job accidents than Quiot and 2) that experts say that sleep deprivation and fatigue contribute to many on-the-job accidents.

Faulty assumptions

· Quiot is exactly comparable to Panoply Industries

· No factor other than sleep deprivation and fatigue is significant for on-the-job accidents

· The extra hour will be used by workers to sleep and for no other activity

Missing evidence

· Other possible contributing factors to on-the-job accidents

· Proof about how exactly Quiot is comparable to Panoply Industries

Counter-examples

· What if some other factor like unfamiliar machinery or inadequate training is responsible for on-the-job accidents?

· What if Panoply Industries is a completely different type of company, manufacturing something fundamentally different from what Quiot does?

· What if some other factor in Panoply is responsible for fewer on-the-job accidents?

· What if the workers won't use the extra hour to sleep but use it for something else leaving them sleep deprived?

Essay

A VP of a manufacturing company suggests cutting work shifts by one hour each in order to reduce on-the-job accidents. The suggestion has been made on the basis of similar reduction by a nearby company with fewer on-the-job accidents and on belief of experts regarding on-the-job accidents. The argument may seem convincing on initial analysis, but a more detailed evaluation reveals hasty assumptions and lack of evidence.

To begin with, the VP has strung just a list of facts together but not proved the connection, merely assumed them. First, the VP states that Quiot has 30% more on-the-job accidents than Panoply. To reduce these on-the-job accidents, the VP suggests that Quiot reduce its work shifts by one hour because Panoply has done so. This entire proposition relies on two assumptions that Quiot is identical to Panoply and that Panoply has fewer on-the-job accidents because of only one-hour shorter work shifts. These assumptions need proof before the VP can go ahead with his suggestion. If Panoply is a completely different company from Quiot, nothing than Panoply does will necessarily apply to Quiot or have the same effect. They could be as different as chalk and cheese! Even if Panoply and Quiot are comparable, the VP needs to establish that the one-hour shorter work shifts are the direct cause of fewer on-the-job accidents. For all we know, Panoply may have instituted some measures that reduced their on-the-job accidents and their one-hour shorter work shifts are merely a coincidental occurrence. Unless, the VP furnishes concrete evidence proving that one-hour shorter work shifts are responsible for the fewer on-the-job accidents, taking the suggestion seriously becomes difficult.

Furthermore, in a bid to strengthen his proposal, the VP provides some evidence in the form of general belief of experts about on-the-job accidents. However, this evidence is inadequate because the VP fails to mention whether this general belief applies to the manufacturing sector, and specifically to Quiot. Generalizations can never be effective supports of any plan since they do not apply to specific instances. The VP would have made a stronger memo if he had included specific data regarding on-the-job accidents for manufacturing industries.

To conclude, what the VP needs to do is analyze the reasons for higher on-the-job accidents in Quiot, especially factors like new or unfamiliar machinery, insufficient training of the workers, lack of clear protocols for anomalous situations, and any such factors that can affect on-the-job accidents. Likewise, the VP must also ascertain what makes Panoply a safer workplace, either because it is a company with less on-the-job accidents or because it has better training of its workforce. After conducting such investigations, the VP must then formulate a plan of action to tackle the problem. Merely aping Panoply and assuming that the extra hour from work shifts will be used by workers to get extra sleep is not a responsible decision. If the VP keeps these considerations in mind, the argument that is currently vulnerable can be made sound.

6.10   Essay 10 (Jazz music club)

> *The following was written as a part of an application for a small-business loan by a group of developers in the city of Monroe.*
>
> "A jazz music club in Monroe would be a tremendously profitable enterprise. Currently, the nearest jazz club is 65 miles away; thus, the proposed new jazz club in Monroe, the C-Note, would have the local market all to itself. Plus, jazz is extremely popular in Monroe: over 100,000 people attended Monroe's annual jazz festival last summer; several well-known jazz musicians live in Monroe; and the highest-rated radio program in Monroe is 'Jazz Nightly,' which airs every weeknight at 7 P.M. Finally, a nationwide study indicates that the typical jazz fan spends close to $1,000 per year on jazz entertainment."
>
> *Write a response in which you discuss what specific evidence is needed to evaluate the argument and explain how the evidence would weaken or strengthen the argument.*

Understand the argument

A group of developers are applying for a loan to start a small business. These developers plan to open a Jazz Club in Monroe because they feel that such a club will be highly profitable in Monroe. To prove that the club will be profitable they provide various pieces of data: 1) the nearest club is 65 miles away, making the new club they plan to build in Monroe the closest one for Monroe residents; 2) since over 100,000 people attended the Jazz festival in Monroe, Jazz is apparently very popular in Monroe; 3) the best-rated program is Jazz Nightly in Monroe, proving that Jazz is supposedly loved by the people; 4) many famous jazz musicians live in Monroe, implying that Jazz musicians also like Monroe; and 5) a study showed that a jazz fan spends about 1,000 dollars annually on jazz, implying that there's a profitable market for jazz in general.

Claim: A Jazz Club in Monroe will be highly profitable

Faulty assumptions

· Most of the 100,000 people who attended the Jazz festival in Monroe live in Monroe itself and had not come from any other place

· The best-rated program means it's the most loved one by audience, and not just by critics

· There are many average jazz fans who spend 1000 dollars annually living in Monroe

· Monroe residents would visit a Jazz club if it were not 65 miles away

· That well-known Jazz musicians live in Monroe is relevant

Missing evidence

- Details about the people who attended the Jazz festival in Monroe

- Information about how the radio program Jazz Nightly got the highest ratings – by the critics or by the Monroe audience

- Specifics about the actual location of the so-called average jazz fan and details about the 1,000 dollars spent – on clubs and entertainment, or on music tapes, instruments, concerts, merchandise, etc.

- Details about how many Monroe residents visit the club 65 miles away

- Whether the well-known Jazz musicians who live in Monroe get mobbed by Jazz fans from Monroe

Counter-examples

- What if most of the 100,000 people who attended the Jazz festival in Monroe do not live in Monroe itself but had come from other places to attend the Jazz festival?

- What if the radio program Jazz Nightly is best-rated by the critics but not by the Monroe audience?

- What if not many of the average jazz fans reside in Monroe?

- What if the average jazz fans spend most of the 1,000 dollars on concerts, merchandise, etc and not on clubs?

- What if the club 65 miles away has no visitors who are Monroe residents?

- What if the well-known Jazz musicians who live in Monroe live there because no one in Monroe recognizes them or bothers them?

Essay

A group of developers who are applying for a loan to start a small business plans on opening a Jazz Club in Monroe because the developers feel that such a club will be highly profitable. While they may have a good business idea regarding the club, they fail to be convincing because their argument relies on multiple flawed assumptions and provides only partial evidence.

The biggest problem with the argument is the fact that almost every fact that they developers have provided is incomplete and does not provide the entire picture in context, forcing one to make assumptions. The biggest fact used by the developers is that over a 100,000 people attended the Jazz festival in Monroe last summer. However, the argument is conspicuously silent about how many of these 100,000 people actually reside in Monroe. Big festivals, such as Coachella and Comic-Con may be held in different cities and hundreds of thousands who come from all over the country visit those festivals. We cannot simply assume that the 100,000 people attended the Jazz festival in Monroe live in Monroe too. If most of them did live in Monroe, a viable market would be easily available. Next partial evidence is about the radio program Jazz Nightly being the best-rated on in Monroe. Assuming there are no other equally best-rated programs, how can we still be sure that these high ratings imply popularity among audience too? Typically, ratings indicate the preferences of the critics, but not necessarily those of the audience. Without further details on the ratings and reach of the Jazz Nightly, we cannot evaluate this fact as to its relevance. Another hole in the evidence is the partial piece about the study stating that a jazz fan spends about 1,000 dollars annually on jazz, without any specifics whatsoever about where do most of these jazz fans live and on what do they spend their 1,000 dollars. What if no such jazz fan lives in Monroe, and even if some do, they spend the 1,000 dollars not on jazz clubs but on jazz concerts and merchandise? Without such supporting details, the study cannot be factored into the argument. Finally, there are some other random bits of information that seemingly just float about in the argument without making any point. That many well-known Jazz musicians live in Monroe seems hardly relevant to whether a Jazz Club in Monroe will be highly profitable. In fact, this evidence suggests that the well-known Jazz musicians probably live in Monroe because there are not many jazz fans who would recognize the musicians and mob them or bother them! The fact that the closest Jazz club is 65 miles away seems to imply that no Jazz fans live in Monroe, unless we are told that many Monroe residents visit that club.

To sum up, the developers' claims might have been valid had they not based their predictions on incomplete, and therefore flawed, data. If the developers took into account the requirements outlined above, the argument would be far sounder than it is now.

6.11   Essay 11 (Electric power company)

> *The following appeared in a memorandum from the planning department of an electric power company.*
>
> "Several recent surveys indicate that home owners are increasingly eager to conserve energy. At the same time, manufacturers are now marketing many home appliances, such as refrigerators and air conditioners that are almost twice as energy efficient as those sold a decade ago. Also, new technologies for better home insulation and passive solar heating are readily available to reduce the energy needed for home heating. Therefore, the total demand for electricity in our area will not increase—and may decline slightly. Since our three electric generating plants in operation for the past twenty years have always met our needs, construction of new generating plants will not be necessary."
>
> *Write a response in which you examine the stated and/or unstated assumptions of the argument. Be sure to explain how the argument depends on these assumptions and what the implications are for the argument if the assumptions prove unwarranted.*

Understand the argument

The planning department of an electric power company has written a memo in which it has claimed that constructing new generating plants will not be necessary, and that the current plants will continue to meet the needs of the area. This claim is based on the premise that people in the area have become environment-conscious and they are eager to conserve energy. The claim is also given support of the fact that home appliances today, compared to those that were a decade old, are twice as energy efficient. Final piece of evidence given by the planning department to support their claim is that there are energy-saving technologies that reduce the energy consumption in home heating. All these premises are used for the claim that the energy consumption in the area will not increase, might probably decline and thus, constructing new generating plants will not be necessary since the current plants will continue to meet the needs of the area.

Claims: 1) The total demand for electricity in our area will not increase, and 2) constructing new generating plants will not be necessary since the current plants will continue to meet the needs of the area.

Faulty assumptions

- Overall energy consumption has not gone up significantly

- Energy efficient appliances don't induce people into using more energy overall

- The population of the town will not go up significantly

- No new devices are being purchased that could take the energy consumption up significantly

Missing evidence

· Details about the total energy consumption a decade ago and now

· Information about population of the area a decade ago and now

· Whether people own appliances that weren't around a decade ago

Counter-examples

· What if the overall energy consumption of the area has gone up?

· What if the population of the town has gone up significantly?

· What if the people own far more appliances today than they did a decade ago?

Essay

A memo by the planning department of an of an electric power company claims that construction of new generating plants will not be necessary since the current plants will continue to meet the needs of the area. To prove this point, the department has furnished various pieces of data for consideration. Unfortunately, while the planning department could have made a convincing argument, the current one does not have a sound basis because it relies on generalizations and it fails to take into account certain possibilities.

To start with, simply stating that home appliances today, unlike those that were a decade old, are twice as energy efficient proves nothing in this absolute manner, unless information about total energy consumption a decade ago is shown as being double what it is today. For all we know, the fact that the appliances today are more energy-efficient may have lulled people into a sense of saving energy and induced them to actually use more energy than they did earlier by running those appliances for longer periods or buying more such appliances than they did earlier. For example, people buy bigger fridges, more powerful ACs, larger food processors on the assumption that the new appliances are twice as energy-efficient, but end up spending the same amount of energy, possibly more than, they did with the earlier less energy-efficient appliances because the size of the appliances is bigger or the use is longer overall. This fact about energy-efficient appliances also does not take into account introduction of new appliances for home use, appliances that were not even present a decade ago. Almost all households these days have multiple computers or laptops, mobile phones, more than television, tablet devices, and many sundry items that consume energy. These would have definitely increased the total energy consumption of every household. Without factoring in these possibilities, citing energy efficiency is pointless.

Another glaring assumption is the lack of discussion of an imperative fact–the population of the area. Even if all the talk of energy efficiency reducing the overall energy consumption is true, an increase in population will take up the total energy requirement of the area considerably. Omission of such details makes the argument specious.

To conclude, the argument makes claims without sufficient, relevant data. What the planning department should do to improve its claim is asses the changes in population over the past decades, calculate and compare the overall energy consumption a decade ago and now, and ascertain the production capacity of the current plants. Only if this information is found and it shows that the trends suggest no increase in overall energy consumption can we conclude that no new plants need be constructed. For now, whether such new generating plants will be necessary cannot be determined.

6.12 Essay 12 (Sunnyside Towers)

> *The following appeared in a letter from the owner of the Sunnyside Towers apartment complex to its manager.*
>
> "One month ago, all the showerheads in the first three buildings of the Sunnyside Towers complex were modified to restrict maximum water flow to one-third of what it used to be. Although actual readings of water usage before and after the adjustment are not yet available, the change will obviously result in a considerable savings for Sunnyside Corporation, since the corporation must pay for water each month. Except for a few complaints about low water pressure, no problems with showers have been reported since the adjustment. I predict that modifying showerheads to restrict water flow throughout all twelve buildings in the Sunnyside Towers complex will increase our profits even more dramatically."
>
> *Write a response in which you discuss what questions would need to be answered in order to decide whether the prediction and the argument on which it is based are reasonable. Be sure to explain how the answers to these questions would help to evaluate the prediction.*

Understand the argument

An owner of an apartment complex, in a letter to the manager of the complex, claims that modifying showerheads to restrict water flow through the 12 buildings in the complex will increase the profits considerably. The owner of the complex has to pay for the water use of the complex. This claim is based on the consideration that a month ago this plan was carried out in 3 buildings. The flow of water through the shower was 1/3 of what it used to be. The owner acknowledges that he does not have any hard data on actual savings yet. However, the owner is certain that there's a huge saving to be made. Also, the owner states that only a few people have complained about low water pressure, thus implying that the plan will have no significant negative effects.

Faulty assumptions

· Restricting flow of water only to the showerheads will reduce the overall use of water and save money

· Restricting flow of water will not have any repercussions affecting the business

Missing evidence

· Data on overall water consumption before the modification of showerheads and after too

· Feedback on the plan by the residents of the complex to gauge the possible repercussions

Counter-examples

· What if the overall water consumption is the same as before modifying the water flow?

· What if residents don't waste water through showers but waste it through other means such as gardening use or cleaning use?

· What if the word-of-mouth publicity hurts the future prospects of the apartment complex?

Essay

In a letter to the manager of an apartment complex, the owner of the said complex claims to have a plan that would save them considerable amounts of money. The owner provides many assumptions to support his claims. However, the assumptions are not sound and therefore, the claims of the owner regarding the plan are unconvincing.

To begin with, the owner plans to restrict water flow through the 12 buildings by modifying showerheads based on a trial run that has not been completed yet. In the trial run, the plan was carried out in miniature on 3 of those 12 buildings. However, no concrete data on water consumption has been made available yet. Thus, concluding that this plan will save money is yet premature. Unless, we have data on the overall water consumption before and after the modification of showerheads, we cannot even infer that any water at all has been saved, let alone assume that profits will be increased! Even if water consumption has reduced after the modification of showerheads, we need to assess the cost of doing so against the benefit of the move. Assuming that the cost of modifying showerheads was offset by the lower water bill this month, one cannot assume that the trend of water consumption will continue for the months to come, because showers are not the only way people can utilize water! The owner has made a faulty assumption that showers are the only significant way that people use water. What if the people are actually using excessive amounts of water for cleaning their cars or watering grass lawns? Modifying showerheads would then save only a marginal amount of water. Also, the owner just skims over the fact that some people have complained about the low water pressure in these 3 buildings. No mention of the possible negative publicity has been made or measures to deal with such a situation have been discussed.

To strengthen his argument, the owner should first thoroughly evaluate the pattern of water consumption by the people, including the manners in which the people use water – whether to water their gardens or hose down their cars. Next, the owner must determine the choices that are available to reduce wasteful use of water, from running awareness campaigns to modifying all water outlets, instead of just showerheads. After settling upon the correct combination of steps that can be taken, implementation must be done in a phased manner, in steps, over proper time periods that would include seasonal variables. After analysis of those field trials, the owner must determine the success of the plan and assess the possible repercussions. Finally, a plan must be decided to deal with possible negatives and then the final execution of the plan must be carried out with proper planning and contingency measures.

To conclude, the owner has presented a good idea – saving water – even if it is primarily to increase profits. However, the hasty conclusions drawn on the basis of incomplete plans and lack of planning leave the whole plan sullied. If the above factors are taken into consideration, the plan can be quite fruitful. Nevertheless, the current argument is sadly incomplete and unreliable.

6.13   Essay 13 (Milk and dairy products)

"Milk and dairy products are rich in vitamin D and calcium—substances essential for building and maintaining bones. Many people therefore say that a diet rich in dairy products can help prevent osteoporosis, a disease that is linked to both environmental and genetic factors and that causes the bones to weaken significantly with age. But a long-term study of a large number of people found that those who consistently consumed dairy products throughout the years of the study have a higher rate of bone fractures than any other participants in the study. Since bone fractures are symptomatic of osteoporosis, this study result shows that a diet rich in dairy products may actually increase, rather than decrease, the risk of osteoporosis"

Write a response in which you discuss what specific evidence is needed to evaluate the argument and explain how the evidence would weaken or strengthen the argument.

Understand the argument

The given argument claims that a diet rich in dairy products may increase, rather than decrease, the risk of osteoporosis. This claim is based on a long-term study involving many people. This study apparently refutes the general belief that a diet rich in dairy products can help prevent osteoporosis – which causes the bones to weaken significantly with age. The general belief is based on the fact that milk and dairy products are rich in vitamin D and calcium, therefore, substances essential for building and maintaining bones. This study has supposedly disproved the general belief because people who consistently consumed dairy products throughout the years of the study have a higher rate of bone fractures than any other participants in the study and fractures are indicative of osteoporosis.

Claim:A diet rich in dairy products may increase, rather than decrease, the risk of osteoporosis; the general belief that diets rich in dairy products can help prevent osteoporosis is untrue.

Faulty assumptions

· No factor significantly affected bone health in the participants of that study

· Consuming dairy products is directly responsible for causing bone fractures in the participants of that study

· All bone fractures in the participants of that study equal osteoporosis for sure

Missing evidence

· Details about other factors that may have impacted bone health in the participants of that study

- Details about what proportion of participants of that study actually developed osteoporosis

- Details about other causes of bone fractures in the participants of that study

- Specific information about how exactly consuming dairy products is directly responsible for causing bone fractures in the participants of that study

Counter-examples

- What if some other factor is responsible for causing bone fractures in the participants of that study?

- What if the bone fractures have not led to osteoporosis in the participants of that study?

- What if some other factor caused weakened bones in the participants of that study?

- What if other people who did not consume dairy products were more vulnerable to osteoporosis?

Essay

The given argument claims that a diet rich in dairy products, instead of decreasing the risk of osteoporosis, may in fact increase it. This claim is based on the details of a study. On initial analysis the argument may seem convincing but a deeper perusal reveals certain flaws like flawed assumptions and lack of supporting evidence.

To begin with, the argument merely provides a positive correlation between two things as proof that one thing caused another. Just because the participants consumed dairy products and were more prone to bone fractures does not mean the former caused the latter! Unless one eliminates all other possible factors that may have contributed to reduced bone health, one cannot suggest that consuming dairy causes bone fractures, and ultimately leads to osteoporosis. In fact, even if one does not consider other factors, it is highly unlikely that dairy products that are rich in vitamin D and calcium could ever hurt bone health. The maximum one can infer is that despite consuming such products, which help the bones, some other factor's influence may have been so much worse that these products could not improve bone health. The argument should have proved the claimed connections without assuming them to be true.

Another flaw in the argument is the lack of analysis of several other factors in diet and environment that could impact bones, leaving them vulnerable to fractures. Many genetic, dietary and environmental causes can lower bone density. Lifestyle choices such as smoking and drinking also increase the chances of lower bone density. Studies show that if a person does not consume the requisite amount of magnesium, absorbing vitamins and calcium becomes difficult. Any of these could have caused the increased fractures in the participants of that study and the argument completely leaves such possibilities out. Also, the argument does not even provide proper details about the actual condition of the participants of that study. The argument simply states that the participants that ate more dairy products were more prone to bone fractures and that bone fractures are indicative of osteoporosis. However, the argument does not specify whether those participants actually developed osteoporosis. Thus, without this information, making conclusions about osteoporosis seems hasty and illogical.

In conclusion, the argument leaves out several key points of information, assumes a cause and effect relationship without proving it and jumps to an unwarranted conclusion. As a result, the argument is utterly unconvincing and unreasonable.

6.14 Essay 14 (Crust Copper Company)

> *The following appeared in a letter to the editor of a journal on environmental issues.*
>
> "Over the past year, the Crust Copper Company (CCC) has purchased over 10,000 square miles of land in the tropical nation of West Fredonia. Mining copper on this land will inevitably result in pollution and, since West Fredonia is the home of several endangered animal species, in environmental disaster. But such disasters can be prevented if consumers simply refuse to purchase products that are made with CCC's copper unless the company abandons its mining plans."
>
> *Write a response in which you examine the stated and/or unstated assumptions of the argument. Be sure to explain how the argument depends on these assumptions and what the implications are for the argument if the assumptions prove unwarranted.*

Understand the argument

In a letter to the editor of a journal on environmental issues, a writer asks consumers to not buy products made with CCC's copper. The reason for this claim is that the copper will come from mining in West Fredonia, a tropical country with endangered animals. CCC's mining will cause pollution and put those animals in danger; unless the consumers don't buy CCC's copper to prevent CCC from mining.

Claim: Don't buy products made with CCC's copper to save environment and endangered animal species.

Faulty assumptions

- If consumers don't buy CCC's copper, CCC will stop mining.

- It is possible for a consumer to tell which product contains CCC's copper

- CCC sells copper products only to consumers and does not sell any significant amount to other companies

- No other method of mining can prevent pollution

- CCC intends to mine copper in West Fredonia

Missing evidence

- Details about CCC's sale of mined copper; to whom it sells and whether it's possible for a consumer to identify something made with CCC's copper

- Methods of mining and possible solutions to prevent pollution while mining

- Information about a way of mining copper but saving the endangered animals

- CCC's plans for the land in West Fredonia

Counter-examples

- What if even after consumers don't buy CCC's copper, the mining carried out up to that point results in extinction of those endangered animals?

- What if consumers cannot identify which product contains CCC's copper?

- What if copper mining can be done without causing pollution or endangering animals?

- What if CCC does not sell its copper to consumers but sells it to companies who use that copper as a raw material and these companies refuse to not buy CCC's copper?

- What if CCC plans to use the land for some other purpose?

Essay

A letter to the editor of a journal on environmental issues exhorts consumers to not buy any products made with CCC's copper because CCC is apparently going to put endangered animals at risk by mining in West Fredonia. While the letter raises some valid concerns, its claims smack of hasty and ill-constructed logic, leaving the whole argument unreasonable.

To begin with, the entire discussion may turn out to be a moot point, if it is found out that CCC never intended to mine copper in West Fredonia. Simply stating that CCC, which admittedly is a copper company, has purchased 10,000 square miles in West Fredonia does not by default mean that it intends to mine copper there. It could very well have bought that land only to put up a processing plant or to enter a new market there. The letter should have explicitly specified CCC's intentions with the land in West Fredonia.

Another big flaw in the entire argument is the hasty assumption that mining always causes pollutions and puts endangered animals at risk. What if some method of mining minimizes the impact on the ecosystem to the extent that endangered animals remain relatively safe? Or, perhaps, CCC is aware of possible repercussions of mining and taking measures to protect those animals and reduce pollution, measures such as biosphere enclosures, effluent treatment, etc. One needs to inspect CCC's track record so far and see how it has fared in eco-consciousness before automatically tagging it as environmentally insensitive.

Finally, before urging all consumers to not buy products made with CCC's copper, the writer of the letter should have determined whether it is possible for a consumer to ascertain which products contain CCC's copper. What if CCC itself does not make any products with the mined copper but sells it to various other producers who use it to make all and sundry items? A consumer cannot stop buying every little item from wires to hoses that contain those wires! Information about buyers of CCC's copper would have improved the argument.

To conclude, the concern demonstrated towards the argument in the letter is good and important. However, it is marred by hasty assumptions and unsubstantiated claims. Specifics along the lines discussed above would help the argument considerably and possibly provide a way forward. Nevertheless, the argument is unsound and unconvincing in its current state.

6.15   Essay 15 (Alpaca overcoat)

The following appeared in a memo from the new vice president of Sartorian, a company that manufactures men's clothing

"Five years ago, at a time when we had difficulties in obtaining reliable supplies of high quality wool fabric, we discontinued production of our alpaca overcoat. Now that we have a new fabric supplier, we should resume production. This coat should sell very well: since we have not offered an alpaca overcoat for five years and since our major competitor no longer makes an alpaca overcoat, there will be pent-up customer demand. Also, since the price of most types of clothing has increased in each of the past five years, customers should be willing to pay significantly higher prices for alpaca overcoats than they did five years ago, and our company profits will increase."

Write a response in which you discuss what specific evidence is needed to evaluate the argument and explain how the evidence would weaken or strengthen the argument.

Understand the argument

The new VP of a men's clothing company suggests that the company should start making alpaca overcoats, as the company once did five years ago. The company had stopped doing so because it could not find a reliable fabric supplier. The VP states that now they have a new fabric supplier. The reason the VP thinks the alpaca overcoats will sell is that the company has not offered these for five years and even the competitors stopped making them. The VP feels that there will be some pending demand for alpaca overcoats. Another support the VP adds is that the company can charge considerably higher prices for alpaca overcoats because over the past five years the prices of most types of clothing has gone up.

Claim: Company profits will increase if the company starts offering alpaca overcoats again

Faulty assumptions

· There is still significant demand for alpaca overcoats

· The competitors stopped making alpaca overcoats for reasons other than lack of demand

· Other clothing items are comparable to alpaca overcoats, thereby ensuring the higher prices for alpaca overcoats too

· The new fabric supplier is reliable enough to supply high quality fabric on a regular basis

Missing evidence

- Information about consumer demand for alpaca overcoats

- Details about why the competitors stopped making alpaca overcoats

- Proof how exactly are alpaca overcoats comparable to other clothing items whose prices have increased over the past five years

- Whether the new fabric supplier can be relied upon

Counter-examples

- What if the competitors stopped making alpaca overcoats because of insignificant consumer demand for alpaca overcoats?

- What if consumers aren't willing to pay higher prices for alpaca overcoats?

- What if new fabric supplier is not reliable and does not provide high quality fabric consistently?

Essay

In a memo, the new VP of a men's clothing company suggests that the company begin offering a particular product like it used to five years ago, on the basis of some production updates as well as some assumptions about the market and consumer demands for the said product. While the new VP is probably pitching a good plan, the lack of thorough substantiation for the assumptions employed in the argument leave his plan flawed.

To begin with, when the VP suggests that the company start making alpaca overcoats again, he simply assumes that consumer demand for alpaca overcoats is significant, without determining the same. In fact, the premise that the VP presents to suggest that there is some unfulfilled demand for alpaca overcoats seems to imply the opposite! Specifically, the VP states that the major competitor of the company has stopped making these coats, and suggests that there's pent-up demand, since alpaca overcoats weren't being offered. However, this same fact that major competitor of the company has stopped making these coats can imply that there was no consumer demand to cater to, thus making companies stop offering alpaca overcoats, per the market forces. The VP should have provided information that could conclusively prove that demand for alpaca overcoats is significant, by way of market surveys. Also, the VP should have discussed the specific reason the major competitor stopped making the coats to negate the possibility that there's no consumer demand.

Furthermore, the VP mentions certain other things that can be interpreted in more ways than one, leading to unwarranted assumptions. One of these is the fact that the company stopped making alpaca overcoats only because it could not find a reliable fabric supplier of high quality wool fabric, but it can start again now because it has a new fabric supplier, leading to the assumption that this new supplier is reliable enough to provide high quality wool fabric in a consistent manner. Without ascertaining the credentials of the new supplier, this exercise cannot be undertaken. Another fact that the VP takes for granted is that because the prices of most other clothing items have gone up, assuming people still want alpaca overcoats, one can charge higher prices for those coats. Unless it is established that alpaca overcoats are comparable to those most other clothing items, assuming higher prices can be charged is unsound.

To conclude, the VP can improve his suggestion of reintroducing a new product into the market, thereby making the company more popular and profitable, if he takes into account the various assumptions that need buttressing with specific details, as discussed above. The idea can be a good one, upon thorough research before implementation. All the same, as it stands, the current argument is unconvincing.

6.16 Essay 16 (Island of Tria)

> *The following is a letter to the head of the tourism bureau on the island of Tria.*
>
> "Erosion of beach sand along the shores of Tria Island is a serious threat to our island and our tourist industry. In order to stop the erosion, we should charge people for using the beaches. Although this solution may annoy a few tourists in the short term, it will raise money for replenishing the sand. Replenishing the sand, as was done to protect buildings on the nearby island of Batia, will help protect buildings along our shores, thereby reducing these buildings' risk of additional damage from severe storms. And since beaches and buildings in the area will be preserved, Tria's tourist industry will improve over the long term."
>
> *Write a response in which you discuss what specific evidence is needed to evaluate the argument and explain how the evidence would weaken or strengthen the argument.*

Understand the argument

In a letter to the head of tourism bureau of Tria, the author claims that tourists should be charged for the use of beach to generate money to replenish the sand as a resolution to the erosion of beach sand. This claim is based on the requirement that tourism industry and buildings along our shores are under the threat due to erosion of beach sand. The claim is supported by the premise that the nearby island of Batia did the same to achieve the said goals. This move is also supposed to reduce these buildings' risk of additional damage from severe storms. The author has also stated that he expects some negative feedback on the move of charging for the use of beach, but says that this move is beneficial over the long term.

Claim: Charge the tourists for the use of beach to generate money to replenish the sand

Faulty assumptions

- Batia is completely comparable to Tria

- Charging for the use of beach will not significantly affect the tourism in Tria

- Replenishing the sand will not necessitate charging the tourists continuously

- Erosion of beach sand will not occur after replenishing the sand

- No other viable way to replenish the sand

- No other viable way to stop or reverse erosion of beach sand

Missing evidence

- Proof about how exactly is Batia comparable to Tria

- Details about the impact of charging for the use of beach will affect tourism

- Whether erosion of beach sand will stop after replenishing the sand

- The details about why exactly erosion of beach sand occurred

- Whether the tourists will need to be charged regularly if replenishing the sand will be required frequently

- Whether money can be generated in some other manner

- Whether any alternative method can solve the problem of erosion of beach sand

Counter-examples

- What if Batia's and Tria's reasons for erosion are completely different?

- What is Batia is completely different from Tria?

- What if charging for the beach use negatively impacts the tourism industry over the long term?

- What if replenishing is required frequently, necessitating charging the tourists routinely, affecting the tourism?

- What if erosion can be stopped or reversed without replenishing the sand?

- What if erosion continues after replenishing the sand?

Essay

In a letter to the head of tourism bureau of Tria, the writer presents a suggestion in a bid to resolve a problem being faced by the island of Tria. As support for his suggestion, the writer furnishes some premises based on comparisons and observations. While the suggestion may have some grain of logic in it, its reliance on assumptions and its lack of adequate evidence leaves the argument flawed.

To begin with, the author suggests that tourists should be charged for the use of beach to generate money to help the tourism in the island, and even acknowledges that this move will create some negative effects, but fails to prove that this move will not overall harm less and help more the tourism industry in the long run. This move may end up annoying more than just a few tourists, in which case, the entire tourism industry may get affected in a big way. Without knowledge of possible repercussions, this move cannot be implemented. Some trial runs should have been conducted and tourists should have been surveyed.

Further, this plan's success has been predicted using Batia's case for an apparently similar situation. However, the author has not bothered to substantiate this prediction by explaining the similarities between Batia and Tria, and more importantly, the exact comparability between Batia's problem of erosion of beach sand and that of Tria. Instead of merely stating that Batia had a problem with erosion of beach sand, as does Tria, and that Tria should follow Batia's method, the author should have investigated the problem and found its cause. After finding the cause of erosion of beach sand, the author should have provided a comparison of all possible alternatives to deal with the problem and the implications of each of those resolutions. Simply aping Batia may not even solve the problem is the causes are different! Also, evaluating all possible solutions may find a way in which tourists need not be charged at all, leaving the tourism industry intact.

Finally, another point that the author fails to consider is that even if we assume that the only way to solve the problem of the erosion of beach sand is by replenishing the sand, charging tourists for the use of beach may end up being a temporary solution, especially if the cause of the erosion remains unaddressed and replenishing needs to be done frequently. It is reasonable to assume that tourists may not mind much if the charging is to be done on a temporary basis; however, if it is meant to be a permanent move, to replenish the sand on a regular basis, the tourism industry may get a fatal blow! Also, issues such as the exact mechanism of charging will then need to be ascertained. Public goods such as parks, beaches, etc. are used by different people to different extent for a variety of needs. Charging everyone the same is unfair, and charging in a differential manner is impractical. None of this has been considered by the writer.

To conclude, there are some major lapses in the reasoning on the part of the writer. The author fails to consider various aspects and presents a hastily constructed solution. Had the author taken into consideration all the possibilities discussed above, the argument would have been stronger than it is now.

6.17   Essay 17 (Humana University)

The following is part of a memorandum from the president of Humana University.

"Last year the number of students who enrolled in online degree programs offered by nearby Omni University increased by 50 percent. During the same year, Omni showed a significant decrease from prior years in expenditures for dormitory and classroom space, most likely because instruction in the online programs takes place via the Internet. In contrast, over the past three years, enrollment at Humana University has failed to grow, and the cost of maintaining buildings has increased along with our budget deficit. To address these problems, Humana University will begin immediately to create and actively promote online degree programs like those at Omni. We predict that instituting these online degree programs will help Humana both increase its total enrollment and solve its budget problems."

Write a response in which you discuss what questions would need to be answered in order to decide whether the prediction and the argument on which it is based are reasonable. Be sure to explain how the answers to these questions would help to evaluate the prediction.

Understand the argument

In a memo, the president of Humana University recommends that Humana should start offering online courses, the way Omni has done last year. The reason for offering online courses is to try to increase total enrollments and to decrease budget deficit. The enrollments have remained steady over the past three years, but the maintenance costs have increased. To prove that the plan would have the desired result, the president cites various premises. The primary support is the fact that the number of online enrollments increased by 50% for Omni University and that the maintenance costs of Omni University's dorm and classes decreased. The president predicts that offering online courses will increase Humana's total enrollments and decrease budget deficit, by bringing in more money.

Claim: Offering online courses will increase total enrollments and decrease budget deficit

Faulty assumptions

- Budget deficit will decrease if more students enroll for online courses

- Offering online courses will not affect enrollment for classroom courses at Humana University

- Setting up online courses will not significantly increase costs for Humana

- Omni and Humana are comparable to each other

- Increased enrollments in online courses is directly responsible for deceased maintenance costs for Omni

- 50% increase is significant increase in numbers too

Missing evidence

- Proof of how exactly is Omni comparable to Humana

- Details about other factors that may affect maintenance costs in both Omni and Humana

- Specifics about the planned online offerings of Humana and how it will increase total enrollments

Counter-examples

- What if Omni and Humana are completely different and therefore have incomparable maintenance costs?

- What if Omni university's courses can be converted into online courses but Humana's can't be?

- What if Omni's maintenance costs decreased for reasons other than online courses?

- What if Omni's total enrollments did not increase significantly?

- What if Humana's total enrollments don't increase significantly?

Essay

In a memo, the president of Humana University suggests that Humana University start offering online courses, just as Omni University has done from last year. While the plan looks promising at first glance, the objectives it is meant to achieve seem misaligned, because they rely on faulty assumptions and lack of evidence.

To begin with, the president's primary reason for offering online courses is to increase total enrollments and decrease the budget deficit–both of which are important objectives; however, the reasons cited for these goals are rather a stretch. The president seems to imply that total enrollments need to be increased because enrollments have remained the same over the last three years but the maintenance costs have increased and the budget deficit has increased. So, if enrollments are increased more money will come in and that can reduce the budget deficit. This plan is not quite sound. Total enrollments should be increased as a natural progressive step, and offering online courses seems like the best next step in this technological age. However, only using that planned extra money to plug the budget deficit sounds like evading the task. What the president should do is specifically outline why exactly the budget deficit and the maintenance costs have increased and discuss alternatives to cut back on expenditure. It is quite likely that Omni University must have done something along the lines of such a plan of cutting back spending that reduced its maintenance costs. It is difficult to believe the president's implication that Omni's maintenance costs decreased because its enrollment for online courses increased by 50 percent.

This brings us to the next flaw in the president's plan. Instead of conducting a market survey, researching the courses that Omni and other universities provide online, and evaluating the potential reduction in classroom courses because of the prospect of online ones, the president merely chooses to predict the increase in total enrollments by stating that Omni's enrollment for online courses increased by 50 percent. How does that prove the prediction that Humana's total enrollment will also increase? Unless the president proves that Omni and Humana are completely comparable, and probably do not end up poaching each other's enrollments, and that Omni's total enrollments increased after it started offering online courses, we cannot assume that Humana's total enrollments will increase significantly! Even if we do assume that Humana's total enrollments will increase, the president simply assumes that the extra revenue will reduce the budget deficit, implying that cost of setting up the online courses and maintaining them has not been accounted for.

To conclude, the idea of setting up online courses is excellent. However, if done in a hasty manner, it will end up full of problems. Also, if the idea is used only to generate extra revenue to deal with the budget deficit, full justice may not be done to the concept of online courses. Online courses are the next step for most universities, especially to widen their reach and increase their scope. Such courses also help people, who hitherto would not have been able to afford education or manage the time required, get educated. To hastily implement this idea in the manner suggested by the president of Humana University is illogical. If the president takes into account the nuances of both offering online courses and dealing with increased budget deficit and maintenance costs, the argument would be far more convincing than it is now.

6.18   Essay 18 (Clearview town)

> *The following appeared in a magazine article about planning for retirement*
>
> "Clearview should be a top choice for anyone seeking a place to retire, because it has spectacular natural beauty and a consistent climate. Another advantage is that housing costs in Clearview have fallen significantly during the past year, and taxes remain lower than those in neighbouring towns. Moreover, Clearview's mayor promises many new programs to improve schools, streets, and public services. And best of all, retirees in Clearview can also expect excellent health care as they grow older, since the number of physicians in the area is far greater than the national average."
>
> *Write a response in which you discuss what specific evidence is needed to evaluate the argument and explain how the evidence would weaken or strengthen the argument.*

Understand the argument

In a magazine, an article, to plan about retirement, a writer claims that Clearview is the best choice for retirees. The main supports for this claim are 1) Clearview has natural beauty and climate, 2) Housing is cheaper than it was last year, 3) Taxes are lower than those in nearby towns, 4) the mayor has various town improvement plans, and 5) the number of physicians is higher than the average number in the country.

Claim: : Clearview is the best choice for retirees

Faulty assumptions

· Natural beauty and consistent climate are some of the significant factors considered by retirees

· Number of physicians is directly relevant to quality of health care

· Older people prefer to live in houses and not in retirement homes

Missing evidence

· Amenities specifically addressing the needs of older people

· Details about quality of health care, specifically for older people

· Whether there are good quality retirement homes

Counter-examples

· What if there are good quality retirement homes for old people?

· What if the physicians are not equipped for old people's needs?

· What if the housing costs are lower but cost of living in Clearview is high?

· What if there are no good caretakers for old people to hire?

· What if other support services specially required by old people are not available?

Essay

In a magazine article, an author makes the bold claim that Clearview is the best place for retirees based on many supporting premises. Unfortunately, the premises provided to support this claim do not end up dealing with all possible factors that would concern a prospective retiree, thereby making the claim hasty and incomplete.

To begin with, the author merely cites some facts about Clearview but does not tailor it to apply to retirees. The first fact that Clearview has natural beauty and consistent climate is not necessarily a boon only for older people. Another such fact missing context is that housing cost is lower than that in past year. What if housing cost is higher than that of other cities? Comparative data is given only for taxes but not for housing cost. Finally, another piece of incomplete support is that the number of physicians is higher than the national average. Even if that is so, one cannot assume that the quality of physicians is satisfactory, and that the physicians are capable of dealing with specific geriatric needs.

Furthermore, the author fails to mention various important factors that an older, retiring person would want information about. When the author presented facts about housing cost, he assumed that older people would want to know only about the housing options, and did not address the need of those retirees who would want to not live by themselves but want to move into a retirement home. Not all retirees want the hassle of having to maintain a house. The retirees who would be interested in a house would want to know choices of help available, ranging from daily help to live-in full time help. Also, some old people need to rely on caretakers, about which no information is given. Additionally, even if we assume that the number of physicians is adequate; details are missing about whether the physicians can handle specialized, geriatric needs. Deciding to settle on Clearview would be difficult for retirees without these.

To conclude, the author should have taken into consideration the special needs of retirees and older people and provided appropriate and suitable facts. Just stating some incomplete and partly irrelevant facts does not support the claim that is being made in the argument. Had the author taken into consideration the aspects mentioned above, the argument would have been far more convincing than it is now.

6.19   Essay 19 (Scent of lavender flowers)

An ancient, traditional remedy for insomnia—the scent of lavender flowers—has now been proved effective. In a recent study, 30 volunteers with chronic insomnia slept each night for three weeks on lavender-scented pillows in a controlled room where their sleep was monitored electronically. During the first week, volunteers continued to take their usual sleeping medication. They slept soundly but wakened feeling tired. At the beginning of the second week, the volunteers discontinued their sleeping medication. During that week, they slept less soundly than the previous week and felt even more tired. During the third week, the volunteers slept longer and more soundly than in the previous two weeks. Therefore, the study proves that lavender cures insomnia within a short period of time.

Write a response in which you discuss what specific evidence is needed to evaluate the argument and explain how the evidence would weaken or strengthen the argument.

Understand the argument

The author of the argument claims that lavender-scent treats insomnia, as has been thought traditionally. To prove this claim, the author presents a 3-week study involving 30 volunteers with insomnia who were made to sleep with lavender-scented pillows. In the first week, when the volunteers took their medication, they slept but awoke tired. So, lavender had not had any effect then. In the second week, the medication was stopped, and they slept worse and felt more tired. So, the lavender still had not had any effect. Finally, in the third week, with no medication, the volunteers slept on the same pillows, and they slept longer and better than they did in the previous two weeks. This proves that lavender-scent had curing effect on insomnia.

Claim: Lavender-scent is an effective treatment for insomnia

Faulty assumptions

- 30 is a sufficiently representative number to study the effect of lavender-scent on insomnia.

- Lavender-scent is directly responsible for longer, more sound sleep of the volunteers

- Stopping the sleep medication is not responsible for longer, more sound sleep of the volunteers

- No other factor was responsible for better sleep quality of the volunteers in the third week

- That the lavender-scent worked only in the 3rd week out of 3 weeks is sufficient to prove that it will be effective always in general

Missing evidence

- Whether these 30 volunteers are sufficient to prove lavender-scent effective for insomniacs in general

- How exactly does lavender-scent affect sleep quality and whether it can be used instead of medication

- Other factors that may affect sleep quality in those volunteers

Counter-examples

- What if these volunteers are not representative of insomniacs in general?

- What if some other factor affects sleep quality in those volunteers?

- What if lavender-scent has got nothing to do with better sleep in those volunteers?

- What if stopping the medication led to better sleep in those volunteers?

- What if the tiring 2 weeks of low quality sleep itself resulted in better sleep in the third week?

- What if the use of lavender-scent worked only as a one-time therapy and would have diminishing returns over time?

Essay

In the given argument, the author claims to have proved a traditional belief that lavender-scent is a good treatment for insomnia. The author uses a 3-week study to prove this claim. However, the study does not serve as sufficient evidence, leaving faulty assumptions and incomplete substantiation as the basis and making the argument flawed.

To begin with, the author cites the study as conclusive proof that lavender-scent is effective to treat insomnia, but assumes that a positive correlation between two factors does not necessarily prove that one factor (lavender-scent) is the cause of the other factor (better sleep in those volunteers). Just stating that two things occurred simultaneously does not make it a cause and effect relationship. Any number of multiple factors could have caused the better sleep in those volunteers in the third week.

Furthermore, the study itself seems dubious and does not adequately make any point. In the first week, the study includes both lavender-scent and sleep medication, in which case it is difficult to judge which factor – scent or medication – had the sound but not restorative sleep. Then, in the second week, the medication was stopped but the lavender-scent was continued, despite which the result was poor sleep. The lack of effect of lavender-scent on sleep in this week has not been dealt with. Finally, in the third week, the medication was discontinued but the scent was continued, and sleep was better than it was in the previous two weeks. Two points haven't been considered in the observation in the third week. One point is whether any other new factor was introduced or stopped that may have improved sleep quality, for example, simply the fatigue from the previous two weeks could have led to better sleep in the third week! If the study had continued into the fourth week with similar conditions as the third week, the results would have implied that the lavender-scent improved sleep quality. The second point that has not been considered for the observation in the third week is that better sleep does not necessarily mean good sleep. Simply stating that sleep was better leaves open the possibility that the sleep, by itself, was still not very good. If the author had discussed parameters by which the sleep was evaluated, compared it to sleep quality of non-insomniacs, the claim would have been strengthened.

To conclude, the author needs to prove the cause-and-effect relationship by better analysis and not by showing a positive correlation. Also, the author needs to address other possible factors that can impact sleep quality. Such as stress levels, dietary and environmental factors, etc. Finally, the author needs to widen the scope of the study, as relying on merely 30 people and observations over 3 weeks is hardly sufficient to prove something universally. If the author had taken into considerations these numerous alternative possibilities, the claim would have been far stronger than it is now.

6.20   Essay 20 (Corpora's citizens)

The following appeared in a health magazine published in Corpora.

"Medical experts say that only one-quarter of Corpora's citizens meet the current standards for adequate physical fitness, even though twenty years ago, one-half of all of Corpora's citizens met the standards as then defined. But these experts are mistaken when they suggest that spending too much time using computers has caused a decline in fitness. Since overall fitness levels are highest in regions of Corpora where levels of computer ownership are also highest, it is clear that using computers has not made citizens less physically fit. Instead, as shown by this year's unusually low expenditures on fitness-related products and services, the recent decline in the economy is most likely the cause, and fitness levels will improve when the economy does."

Write a response in which you examine the stated and/or unstated assumptions of the argument. Be sure to explain how the argument depends on these assumptions and what the implications are for the argument if the assumptions prove unwarranted.

Understand the argument

In an article in a health magazine in Corpora, a writer claims that the decline in the economy and not computer ownership is responsible for lower fitness levels in Corpora. The background given about this claim is that levels of physical fitness today are lower than what they were twenty years ago (specifically, twenty years ago, half the people in Corpora were deemed fit, whereas today only a quarter are deemed so). The writer states that experts claim that this reduced level of physical fitness is caused by increased use of computers. However, the writer challenges this claim and states instead that computer ownership is not responsible for lower fitness levels, but the decline in the economy is. To support his claim, the writer provides a fact that in areas of Corpora where levels of physical fitness are highest, levels of computer ownership are also the highest.

Claim: The decline in the economy and not computer ownership is responsible for lower fitness levels in Corpora

Faulty assumptions

· Decline in physical fitness has not been caused by any other factor

· Physical fitness standards have not changed significantly over the past twenty years

· Computer ownership is directly responsible for high fitness levels in parts of Corpora

- Low expenditures on fitness-related products and services mean that the economy is responsible for lower levels of physical fitness

- The people who own computers are the ones who have high levels of physical fitness in those specific regions of Corpora with high levels of physical fitness

- Computer ownership is equivalent to use of computers

Missing evidence

- Details about standards of physical fitness twenty years ago and now

- Proof about how computer ownership is responsible for high fitness levels

- Proof about how decline in the economy is responsible for lower fitness levels

- Specifics about other aspects that may affect levels of physical fitness

- Details about the people who own computers and those who have high levels of physical fitness in those specific regions of Corpora with high levels of physical fitness

Counter-examples

- What if the standards of physical fitness have changed considerably now from what they were twenty years ago, thereby reducing the number of people categorized as physically fit now, as opposed to twenty years ago?

- What if some factor other than computer ownership is responsible for high fitness levels?

- What if some factor other than decline in the economy is responsible for lower fitness levels?

- What if people who own computers in fact have lower levels of physical fitness?

Essay

In a magazine article, a writer claims to disprove the interpretation offered by experts about a piece of fact regarding levels of physical fitness. The writer provides some background information about the levels of physical fitness now and twenty years ago and supports his claim and disproves the experts' by furnishing evidence from certain parts of Corpora. While the claim may seem valid on initial evaluation, but a more detailed analysis reveals lack of relevant evidence and displays many flawed assumptions.

To begin with, the author ends up trying to prove his point and disprove that of experts, without even bothering to check whether any contentious issue exists. Specifically, the apparent contention is the fact that twenty years ago, half the people in Corpora were deemed fit according to standards followed then, whereas today only a quarter are deemed so per today's standards. The fact that the measuring standards are different itself should be a clue that the proportion of people deemed fit in these two different time frames will be vastly different. For all we know, if we were to judge today?s citizens by standards of twenty years ago, we may find a half or more than a half with high levels of physical fitness! One cannot have different frames of measurement to compare any specific thing. Unless this, aspect has been dealt with, to even consider whether fitness levels have changed is ludicrous!

Furthermore, even if we assume that levels of physical fitness of physical fitness have changed, it seems reasonable to state that increasing use of computers may have had some part to play in it, given that internet has almost replaced outside games as pastime. To prove that computers are not responsible for declining levels of physical fitness, the writer provides the fact that in areas where computer ownership is the highest, the people with highest levels of physical fitness are present, without even proving that those people who own these computers are the fittest people being discussed, let alone the fact that merely owning a computer and being fit at the same time does not conclusively prove that increasing use of computer may or may not affect levels of physical fitness! Then to claim that, since expenditures on fitness-related products and services, the decline in the economy has caused the reduced levels of physical fitness. Two events happening together do not necessarily make a cause-and-effect sequence, and could just as easily be a coincidence. The whole claim falls apart, under the slightest evaluation of the supporting premises.

To conclude, what the writer should have done is ascertained the levels of physical fitness of the citizens by a singular frame of reference. After determining the change in the levels of physical fitness, the writer should have considered all possible contributing factors such as dietary, environmental and other lifestyle changes that impact levels of physical fitness. After careful consideration of the same, the writer should then have developed the explanation of the phenomenon in a complex manner. Had the author taken into account the aspects discussed above, the argument would have been far more convincing than it is now.

Chapter 7

Issue Essays

7.1 Essay 1 (Scandals are useful)

> **Scandals are useful because they focus our attention on problems in ways that no speaker or reformer ever could.**
>
> *Write a response in which you discuss the extent to which you agree or disagree with the claim. In developing and supporting your position, be sure to address the most compelling reasons and/or examples that could be used to challenge your position.*

Understand the issue

We have to write an essay in which we state our position on whether scandals are useful because they focus our attention on problems and **speaker or reformer cannot do the same.**

Discussion of the components of the Issue statement

Scandals – Scandals can be widely interpreted. Defining scandals, possibly with examples, before providing a viewpoint is necessary. What are scandals? Events that are widely publicized by the media that get the public's attention and that contain some shock value, probably due to some moral or conventional element in it.

Useful – The extent of usefulness has not been discussed in the issue. How useful? Only in grabbing attention? What about after the attention has been grabbed? Is any desirable outcome achieved after the attention has been focused?

Attention – The duration of attention is worth mentioning. For how long will scandals focus our attention, as opposed to the effect of the same by reformers or speakers?

Problems – The nature of the problems need to be specified. Do scandals focus our attention better than reformers on every type of problem, or are speakers and reformers better in getting our attention on certain issues, while scandals get our attention on some other issues?

No speaker or reformer could – This is too extreme. This is the equivalent of saying that no speaker or reformer could achieve what scandals can. This needs to be included in the essay that speakers and reformers have their own place in the scheme of things while scandals have theirs. To say that one is necessarily better than the other is too extreme.

Some other aspects to be considered

Time frame: This issue needs to be contextualized according to time frame and its impact on the use and reach can be discussed. For example, scandals become global phenomena faster now, than they did before. One can also discuss how people's attitudes towards "scandals" and "reformers" have changed over time. For example, people were easily scandalized earlier, but now are used to sensational news. Equally, these days, not everyone is amenable to the concept of "reformers".

Agree because	Disagree because
Scandals get media attention Eg — Zuckerberg using Ebola	Scandals can also draw attention away from genuine issues and focus them on silly issues Eg — X celebrity visited Y rehab clinic Z celebrity gained/lost XYZ amount of weight
Scandals can put pressure on the authorities to take action even against powerful people Eg — Julian Assange and his WikiLeaks	Scandals can blur the importance of an issue and make attention go away altogether from the issue Eg — the movie Slumdog Millionaire
Scandals have a wider reach	Desensitize people by using strong language which loses impact when used for real problems

Once you have thought of your position (mostly agree/mostly disagree/depends on the situation) and of some examples, start writing the essay. Don't keep brainstorming for too long in an issue task. As you write an essay, new points will come up. Incorporate them into your essay only if you can either explain them well or support them with examples.

Sample Essay (Score 6)

The assertion that scandals help to draw attention towards important issues, more than any reformer or speaker could bring up discussion on scandals themselves. Scandals have been around for as long as human beings have roamed the earth. From the primary scandal of original sin involving Adam and Eve to the most recent one involving any number of Hollywood starlets, scandals have always had the power to catch mankind's attention and generate sparkling debates. Notwithstanding their power to influence the human mind, their usefulness remains debatable. However, comparing usefulness of scandals to that of reformers in getting attention on problems is invalid, because it implies that the scandals and reformers are independent of each other or have no overlap. Also, scandals are not truly comparable to reformers or speakers because they function in different ways, and each has its purpose.

Many people argue that scandals serve no purpose, denigrate discussions by sensationalizing the topic and usually deal only with completely senseless topics that wouldn't have received any attention by anyone remotely intelligent. The same people also argue that such useless scandals also end up making the people jaded about issues and take away the impact value of a "scandal" in general. Regrettably, such scandals do happen, and happen aplenty! To see these scandals at play, all one has to do is turn the TV on and flick to any of the innumerable, so-called "entertainment" channels to find lengthy and highly involved discussions on controversies about celebrities losing or gaining weight, some fashion persona's absurd outfits, or the latest link-ups or break-ups. While these things may serve as "mindless fun" for many, popularizing these takes the attention away from significant things that may have otherwise caught our attention were it not for the desensitizing effect of "silly scandals". After being fed a steady diet of "shocking break-up!" and "amazing weight loss through pills!", any person watching an actually shocking discovery of some big fraud or Ponzi scheme will not feel as moved by either the words or the actual extent of feeling, having experienced the same emotive talk over and over again for inconsequential topics. These people would probably feel that only reformers and speakers can focus public's attention with appropriate seriousness on important issues.

Despite the negatives stacking up against the usefulness of scandals, scandals actually can be extremely powerful as tools, if utilized correctly, to bring about desirable outcomes, such as social change, public empathy, and the power of the masses against the high and mighty. Exactly because of the very sensational nature of scandals, scandals catch attention very quickly, and as long as they are tempered correctly and not allowed to run off on tangents, they can get the usually apathetic public engaged in an important issue. Scandals can not only fetch attention of the public but also whip up public fervor and ensure that some positive measure is implemented. Such a scandal is best demonstrated by the absolute pandemonium that Julian Assange unleashed with Wiki-Leaks, a scandal that put the spotlight on the uncomfortable truths for the US government. Not far behind after that was Snowden's blowing the whistle, and in the process, almost toppling the bureaucratic institutions. In both these examples, scandals helped the underdogs fight off the big, seemingly indomitable sharks by harnessing the power of the collective for these underdogs. Without public uproar, this kind of scrutiny on the governmental institutions would never have been possible, allowing these institutions to feel invincible and free from checks. In such situations, a reformer or a speaker alone would never have garnered this kind of public support or would have probably been censored before reaching the masses.

Furthermore, most scandals have wide reach and can easily penetrate the consciousness of the masses, and usually end up mobilizing the masses in a way that is reminiscent of big revolutions. Consider the Monkey Trial, also known as The Scopes Trial, which brought to attention the whole debate of creationism versus evolution. Admittedly, while it was a blow to the group that wanted science's progress and also on possibly the freedom of speech, the whole scandal brought both sides out in full force, explaining their positions and got the public involved into this discussion, which up to then had been restricted to mostly the elites. Never before this, had actual proper interchange of ideas been done, or had people of both sides come out and acknowledged either side. Without this scandal, the issue would not have progressed further as quickly. Another scandal, quite recently, involving Face-book's founder Mark Zuckerberg and his campaign to generate funding for Ebola, ended up thoroughly publicizing the plight of Ebola patients and collecting a considerable amount for addressing the issue. Up to that point, people were aware of Ebola and the need for money, but still removed from the issue and neutral about it. Zuckerberg's scandal, in which he indeed exonerated himself, made people realize that the Ebola issue is far more important than they had thought. Without this scandal, the lack of concern of people would have been difficult to shake off and no public speaker had been able to excite such phenomenal response from the public up to that point.

To sum up, scandals are always going to be around. Like any other tool, scandals are never good or bad in themselves or necessarily better or worse than reformers or speakers. Whether scandals end up being more useful depends on what the topic of the scandal is and what response has been elicited using those scandals. If they create awareness, evince sympathy about some important issue, then they are definitely useful, probably more so than any reformer could be; on the other hand, if they deal in highlighting the trivial, they are completely useless, and a reformer would do a better job.

Explanation of score 6

The writer of this response sketches a clear and insightful position on the issue and follows the specific instructions by presenting reasons to support that position. The essay logically analyzes the issue and presents a well-balanced opinion that scandals can be both useful and useless. However, scandals do tend to garner public attention well, possibly more than a reformer would. The writer has an engaging way of writing, with sharp and precise vocabulary (evince, elicited, exonerated, phenomenal, mobilizing, indomitable, invincible, etc.). The examples used demonstrate deep and complex thinking about issues and the way these examples have been linked to the given issue prove that the writer has understood the nuances of the issue. The organization is brilliant, with a detailed introduction highlighting the main points of the issue, beginning with the contrary view and finally developing his own position. The response is compelling and persuasive.

Ideas in the essay are connected logically, with effective transitions used both between paragraphs ("However" or "Admittedly", etc.) and within paragraphs. Sentence structure is varied and complex and the essay clearly demonstrates facility with the "conventions of standard written English (i.e., grammar, usage and mechanics)," with only minor errors appearing. Thus, this essay meets all the requirements for receiving a top score a 6.

Sample Essay (Score 5)

The author of the issue claims that scandals are better than reformers at focusing our attention on issues. I must declare that I am neutral on this issue and feel that this statement has both positives and negatives to it. Whether this statement holds true depends on the situation itself and has nothing to do with either scandals or reformers per se. scandals and reformers both can focus attention on the issues as well as worsen the situation for the issue and deflect attention to less important things.

Let's look at situations in which scandals or reformers and speakers have ended up deflecting attention away from the actual issues. Recently, a huge scandal rocked the manufacturing industry, specifically the shoe-makers, in the US. The public had come to know that sports shoes, the supposedly handcrafted shoes that big companies sold for hundreds of dollars, even thousands, were being made by children in Southeast Asian countries for as little as ten or twenty dollars. For quite some time, the outrage was directed not at the fact that American companies are shifting their factories to other countries and employing children, not even at the fact that those same children are being underpaid for the work, but at the fact that shoes made so cheaply are being sold at such a high price to American consumers! It was only when pressure groups and NGOs stepped in and started questioning the whole system of exploiting children that the real issue was brought under discussion. Thus, it took a group of reformers or speakers to get the situation back on the right track, after it had been thrown completely off by scandals. That's not to say that scandals always put the discussion of track and only reformers or speakers get it back on track. However, this is one distinct possibility.

In contrast to this situation, let's look at another situation, in which scandals focused our attention far better than reformers could. Obesity has become an alarming world-wide trend, ever since so called fast food has hit the market. Experts, including reformers and speakers, have been sounding the public off about junk food for decades now, all to very little effect. However, recently, with the advent of internet, news spreads like wildfire. Many junk food scandals have hit the world – from horse meat in burgers, to chicken toes in fried chicken! People have been suitably shocked and horrified. These scandals have done what no reformer ever could – they have brought the whole junk food industry under scrutiny and made people think twice about the repercussions of eating such food. This situation illustrates that sometimes only scandals can focus our attention on issues and shock us out of our inaction, as no reformer or speaker ever could.

To conclude, I reassert my position that one cannot necessarily say that only scandals focus our attention on issues as no reformer could. It cuts both ways equally! Both scandals and reformers and speakers are needed to focus attention and keep it on the right track.

Explanation of score 5

The given essay is strongly logical and extremely well-balanced.

The writer introduces the topic and clearly states his position on the issue. The writer then launches into explaining his position in the body paragraph. The position taken by the author is that this issue can be both agreed and disagreed with. The first body paragraph explains how the writer disagrees with the issue. The point is articulated well with a clear example.

In the second body paragraph, the writer explains how the writer agrees with the issue. Very clear support has been presented for this aspect of the response.

The structure of the essay is quite organized, very well arranged. The conclusion sums up the final and abiding position on the issue.

What keeps this essay from being a score 6 is the rather simplistic language and lack of complex development of ideas. The ideas are strong but not very insightful. The thoughts are good but not excellent. The language is strong but not compelling. The sentence structure is straightforward and repetitive and lacks force.

Thus, the score 5 is for strong, good development of logical ideas and use of correct and partly persuasive language.

Sample Essay (Score 4)

The given issue discusses whether scandals are better at focusing attention of the public. Mostly, it has been seen that scandals are indeed better at getting the attention of the public to things it has been largely ignoring. Thus, I agree with the statement.

To begin with, if we consider scandals and take a look at them, we will find that scandals generally end up revealing all sorts of wrong happenings that were hidden up to that time. For example, a scandal involving some corrupt politician, who is caught taking bribes or displaying favoritism, or a scandal showing government's manipulation of certain media agents, or any of these, end up uncovering wrong things. Once these things have been uncovered, action can be taken against the politician or the government because the public demands it. This wouldn't have happened with a reformer.

While I agree that sometimes, scandals are about useless issues. Sometimes, even when a celebrity or kids of famous people end up doing something normal, a scandal is created and blown out of proportion. People are sometimes excessively concerned about the minute details of lives of famous people and the media exploits this. Nevertheless, without some scandals, no sweeping changes can be achieved. For example, if people had not been scandalized by the actions of oppressors, no freedom revolutions would have ever taken place. If people had not publicized and openly exposed wrong-doers, wrongdoings would not have gotten corrected. Take the example of Lance Armstrong. This huge scandal brought to people?s attention how winners are allowed to get away with anything. However, the strong public reaction will not deter anyone else from doing the same. Reformers or speakers could never have achieved that effect.

Thus, to conclude, scandals are very helpful in implementing big changes and getting the world's attention, mostly better than reformers or speakers can. However, sometimes scandals can be useless too.

Explanation of Score 4

The essay makes some good points with simple organization but lacks consistency.

The writer introduces the issue and states that he agrees with the issue but by the time the essay is through the writer's position seems to have shifted a bit to partly agree and partly disagree with the issue.

That being said, the writer logically analyzes the issue well, presents some good aspects and supports some of those points with examples. However, inconsistency is a big problem throughout. The first body paragraph makes some relevant points, as does the third one, but the second body paragraph seems to be just drifting off topic a bit. Also, the writer does not explain his point well by circling back to his point after discussing his examples. He leaves the reader the task of making connections between his examples and his points.

Organization is satisfactory. There's a clear introduction, body, and conclusion. The language is mostly free of errors and allows comprehension. However, the essay is uninspiring and not compelling at all.

Thus, for simple language, adequate organization and inconsistent but decent logic, a score of 4 has been assigned.

Sample Essay (Score 2)

The given issue claims scandals are very useful because they focus out attention on issues, not like any reformer or speaker can. It is not right Firstly, scandals are a waste of time and money because they never talk about useful things. They are always talking about celebrities and people whom only young people know? Scandals also insult a lot of good people and put fake blame on good people. Scandals are used by bad people to get money and public support. For example, think about the scandal of lindsey lohan or amanda baines going to rehab? These are bad people getting free publicity. What about Iron man's son running from rehab and doing drugs? Why are good people scandalized? All the time, TV channels keep talking about Kim Kardashian and Kanye West and not talking about important things like Eebola in Mexico and Africa? Why dont people know about government frauds and corrupt politicians and bad sportsmen and cheaters? Why dont scandals show all that? Scandals always waste time and don't do good, but hurt good people and help bad people. Scandals can be easily made by paying media. Media these days is not true and honest. Media is also so corrupt. Lastly, reformers are good people and can change people's minds and bring about freedom revolutions. Reformers are good and scandals are bad, so dont comparing them is wrong. Reformers have more impact and speakers too, more then scandals.

Explanation of Score 2

This response is seriously lacking in any sort of analysis and has been given a score 2 largely for lack of consideration and failure to reasonably acknowledge aspects to the issue given. Primarily, the essay position extremely limited in addressing the specific task directions and never explicitly states the extent to which the writer agrees with the issue statement. The flawed reasoning employed and the limited nature of the examples clearly demonstrate that the writer has not understood the statement nor considered the notion of scandals correctly enough. For the most part, the writer seems to have confused the concept of "movie-chat" or "entertainment news" as scandals and spent almost the entire essay criticizing that. Further, the writer also seems rather extremely opinionated against scandals and displays unreasonable position that scandals can never be useful.

The use of language, while comprehensible, is still not grammatical. The writer exhibits that he has no grasp over the distinction between a statement and a question. There are a few spelling errors but those are minor compared to the "questioning sentences" and lack of clear flow. The writer keeps jumping from one concept to another, providing examples and then hopping to something else again.

Overall, the lack of consideration for an alternative opinion, absence of grammar, and shallow examples leave this response unconvincing and lacking depth. In fact, they demonstrate that the writer lacks scientific temper. Thus, an overall score of only 2, mostly because at least the writer has attempted to organize his singular tirade against scandals.

7.2   Essay 2 (Same national curriculum)

> **A nation should require all of its students to study the same national curriculum until they enter college**
>
> *Write a response in which you discuss the extent to which you agree or disagree with the recommendation and explain your reasoning for the position you take. In developing and supporting your position, describe specific circumstances in which adopting the recommendation would or would not be advantageous and explain how these examples shape your position*

Understand the issue

We have to first determine whether we agree that in a country all students must study same syllabus till they enter college. We must provide examples for our position and explain our position with reasoning.

Discussion of the components of issue statement

A nation should – This issue is recommending something to the whole country. The good thing is that the issue says "should" and not "must". Thus, it's only a suggestion, a moral obligation, and not a compulsion. The moral obligation aspect should be discussed. It is best to make suggestions rather than ask for compulsory application.

Require – This word adds compulsion, because "requirement" is not voluntary. This is one of the problems. This aspect needs to be discussed with reference to making it a national and local requirement.

All of its students – This is quite extreme. Whatever the suggestion of the requirement may be, but to apply it to all students, without even checking their inclinations is unfair. Not all students are the same, and therefore, applying anything to everyone is not logical or correct. This sweeping inclusion needs to be discussed in the issue.

To study the same national curriculum – This is again too extreme. All students should study the same curriculum across the whole nation. As a requirement, to force everyone to study the same curriculum without factoring in the differences and specific future plans of different students is extreme. Plus, what will be the national curriculum? This aspect needs to be discussed – what subjects would comprise the national curriculum? At what level – basic, intermediate or advanced – would the curriculum be? What will be the minimum requirements for the students to move on the college? Will college curriculum need modification too, given that all students have studied same syllabus, which may not have been very specialized or technical enough? How this will affect the future of the students needs to be discussed.

Until they enter the college – This aspect makes the whole issue even more extreme. The national curriculum should be made a requirement all the way up to college! If everyone is to study the same curriculum, it will be need to kept general enough. If the students end up studying only in general all the way up to college, how many more years will it take for them to become specialized enough? Professions such as doctor, engineer, architect, etc need to be discussed to show that specialization needs to start earlier. Also, professions such as sportsmen, actors, musicians need to be discussed to factor in those students who need the bare minimum of education. Whether this will delay students from becoming employed needs to be discussed.

Agree because	Disagree because
No student will feel at a disadvantage at the college level	Unfair to make every student study every single thing
Improve standardization of education	Prevents or delays specialization Examples - doctors
Help equitable provision of education	Encourages "jack of all trades, but master of none" attitude
	Takes away the right to make a choice
	Curriculum up to college level will have to be vast to make sure none of the basics are lost, of all possible future fields
	Contains the risk of students not learning all basics for any particular field
	Delays students from getting employed sooner
	Makes even those who don't need to focus on education end up studying the same as everyone else Example - sportsmen
	Impossible to design a desirable and unfair national curriculum

Once you have thought of your position (mostly agree/mostly disagree/depends on the situation) and of some examples, start writing the essay. Don't keep brainstorming for too long in an issue task. As you write an essay, new points will come up. Incorporate them into your essay only if you can either explain them well or support them with examples.

Sample Essay (Score 6)

"Education, then, beyond all other devices of human origin, is the greatest equalizer of the conditions of man" is a bold proclamation by Horace Mann. The author of the given issue seems to have take Horace quite literally! While agreeing with Horace is not that difficult, given that education is the one of the few universal ways to raise oneself to any desirable level, it is nearly impossible to agree with the author, primarily because of the extreme nature of his suggestion and the impracticality of the said suggestion.

To start with the few positives, giving every student same education up to a certain level can help to ensure that everyone is at least educated up to a certain point. It can also be a means to facilitate equitable ordering of society, especially in backward areas. This move could also prevent formation of smaller microcosms of schooling, which inhibit lateral mobility among students of different areas.

Nevertheless, that being said, forcing everyone who wishes to learn, the same curriculum up to the national level is as good as forfeiting democracy and welcoming communism. Taking away a student's right to choose his academic career can only inculcate bitterness in all kinds of students. Let's consider some common professions and the education and training involved in those. Professions such as those of sportsmen, actors, tradesmen, have limited needs for conventional education involving humanities, literature, physical sciences, etc. In the situation that will be created if the author's suggestion is implemented, say, an aspiring sportsman will have to study the national curriculum and then enter college and become a graduate, or forfeit education in favor of his vocational training, and not have a college degree as a backup. If we consider the other end of the spectrum, for profession choices such as doctor, or engineer, a student, in the issue's scenario, will have to study the general national curriculum before entering college and beginning the arduous journey of specialization that is the mark of these professions. How many extra years will be spent before such a student is let loose in his field? Even those in the middle range of the spectrum, people who'd go on to become probably the backbone of an administrative or some bureaucratic system, will end up having to deal with every topic included in the national curriculum, before they graduate, get their job and start learning the ropes of their chosen job.

Moreover, this point of studying the same national curriculum up to the college level brings up the impossibility of designing an unobjectionable national curriculum! This national curriculum will need to be of not too high a level to ensure that every student is able to grasp it. Equally, it will need to cover subjects of all types to provide everyone with a taste of everything to enable the students to judge what the future options are. Further, the curriculum will need to include enough content to make sure that everyone who chooses to pursue whatever college subjects specifically is equipped with the basics of the requisite subjects! Such a combination of diverse subjects with content that is basic enough to not prevent students from crossing over but detailed enough to prepare them for their future needs sounds impossible to create, let alone implement nationally!

Education is one of the fundamental rights of a person. It is meant to provide choices, enabling people to have options in their aspirations, unshackled by race, caste, creed, or economic level. To suggest that this choice be taken away is an extremely unpleasant prospect, preventing the very diversity and uniqueness that marks humanity, and leaving education and uninspiring mix of identical subjects. All students will know the same stuff, through no choice of theirs. What will happen to those wonderful and unique combinations that now throng the schools – the computer nerd who opts for woodwork, or the "fashionista" who chooses multiple languages?

To conclude, the way forward is not to standardize every student up to the same level, but to encourage education, in any form to everyone. Thus, I disagree that all students should be made to study the same curriculum up to the college level, but instead postulate that provisions should be made for everyone to study whatever he or she wishes to, because, education should be as Plutarch quotes, "the mind is not an empty vessel to be filled, but a fire to be kindled".

Explanation of score 6

The writer of this response sketches a clear and insightful position on the issue and follows the specific instructions by presenting reasons to support that position. The essay logically analyzes the issue and presents a well-balanced opinion that scandals can be both useful and useless. However, scandals do tend to garner public attention well, possibly more than a reformer would. The writer has an engaging way of writing, with sharp and precise vocabulary (evince, elicited, exonerated, phenomenal, mobilizing, indomitable, invincible, etc.). The examples used demonstrate deep and complex thinking about issues and the way these examples have been linked to the given issue prove that the writer has understood the nuances of the issue. The organization is brilliant, with a detailed introduction highlighting the main points of the issue, beginning with the contrary view and finally developing his own position. The response is compelling and persuasive.

Ideas in the essay are connected logically, with effective transitions used both between paragraphs ("However" or "Admittedly", etc.) and within paragraphs. Sentence structure is varied and complex and the essay clearly demonstrates facility with the "conventions of standard written English (i.e., grammar, usage and mechanics)," with only minor errors appearing. Thus, this essay meets all the requirements for receiving a top score a 6.

Sample Essay (Score 5)

The given issue brings up a thought that education enlightens the mind as surely as ignorance blinds it. The author of the issue seems to make the issue statement possibly with the intentions of wanting to enlighten minds and improve the overall experience of the students with education, but, regrettably, does not take into account, the most important factor in education of the students, i.e. the students themselves.

To begin, I don't disagree that standardizing the education up to a level does not have its advantages. It can improve quality, control subsystems in the nation, provide consistency, even ensure fairness in a nation's education system. However, standardizing to the extent discussed by the author – up to college level for all students will do far more harm than good, because it overlooks multiple aspects of education.

The primary characteristic of education is that is empowers an individual to become a contributing member of the society. With that duty in mind, education almost always follows the determined career choice. To force the student to learn standardized syllabi all the way up to college, only after which a student can customize his learning as per his chosen profession, is, to say the least, unfair and untenable. No community or nation would concede to such a situation. This would end up either increasing the total number of years a person needs to study before he works or increasing the number of students who drop out halfway through the education to pursue the path of least resistance.

Another aspect of education that should be considered to evaluate the suggestion is the vast nature of it. Educating a student involves introducing him to all aspects of the subjects–mental and physical, garnering his interest into subjects, nurturing his specific talents and supporting him in subjects difficult for him. Thus, different students have vastly different responses to any subject, responses which must be taken into account. Not all subjects should be forced on the students, which can generate an overall dislike for the subject itself. This possible reaction is exactly why many subjects are offered by schools as an optional choice, not as mandatory learning, giving the student some degree of autonomy over his learning. Taking this control away will only hamper the student's development.

Finally, a word must be added over the extent of standardization. Considering a common curriculum up to some basic levels can be a good plan, but forcing it up to college level is not a great idea. In fact, making anything a mandatory requirement, things that are best left as personal choices is not the best move forward.

To conclude, I mostly disagree with the author's recommendation and strongly urge that such choices be left up to the pupils. If any particular subsection wishes to have its curriculum standardized, with the agreement of its people, then so be it. However, to mandate it so is against the basic rights of every individual.

Explanation of score 5

The given response is quite logical and strong but balanced. The writer introduces the topic very well and clearly states his position on the issue. The writer then launches into explaining his position in the body paragraph. The position taken by the author is that this issue can be agreed to up to a certain extent but mostly disagreed with. The first body paragraph explains how the writer agrees with the issue. The point is articulated well with proper supporting details. Then the author launches into why specifically he disagrees with the issue and builds two main paragraphs and a small detailing paragraph on the disagreeing part. The essay does take a complex approach to the issue by developing the issue from many angles and providing appropriate and relevant scenarios to support those points. The author also organizes his essay very well with clear transitions. The author makes use of "appropriate vocabulary and sentence variety." The author does not include some important points in his discussion, such as the difficulty in drafting the kind of standardized curriculum envisaged in the issue.

What keeps this essay from being a score 6 is the rather simplistic language and lack of deeper development of ideas and fewer logical points. The ideas are good but not very insightful. The thoughts are strong but not excellent. The language is correct but not compelling. The sentence structure is straightforward and repetitive and lacks force.

Thus, the score 5 is for strong, good development of logical ideas and use of correct and only partly persuasive language.

Sample Essay (Score 4)

In the given issue, the author discusses implementing a fixed national curriculum for all students until they enter college. This plan has its merits and demerits. I think that to implement this, the nation needs to take a collective decision.

The merits of the plan are that everyone will get standardized education and no one will feel left behind, or at a disadvantage. This move will also prevent any branching of the school systems. If national curriculum is not implemented, then schools and regions have their own syllabus, preventing students from freely moving to newer regions in search of better options. The move will especially help all graduates have a common denominator upon which they can build their future. This equality will further trickle down into the workplace as well and thus foster and overall, harmonious environment and mean well for the future generations.

However, the demerits of the plan are numerous too. To say the least, the plan will extend everyone's education by few years because everyone will need to spend extra years specializing for their jobs. Some may have to spend more than just a few years. This will put extra strain on the people who support the students while they are learning. This will also mean fewer productive years for most workers. Also, not everyone needs specialized education. For example, those who want to eventually just start a farm, don't need to study classroom subjects for so many years. They could be allowed to start their specific learning sooner.

To conclude, the author's suggestion could be implemented if certain factors such as regional requirements are taken into consideration. The issue is a bit extreme but has some good idea in it.

Explanation of Score 4

The writer introduces the issue directly and states his position on it and gets into the issue without much topic development. This response meets all the criteria of a level-4 essay. The writer develops a clear stand – that there are merits and demerits. The position is then developed with relevant reasoning. Though the overall development and organization of the essay does suffer from an attitude of lack of thoroughness (the introduction and conclusion of the essay are too bare and lacking in details and development), the essay as a whole flows smoothly and logically from one idea to the next, starting from general to specific: first a short introduction in which the position has been clearly stated, next the first body paragraph dealing with one side of the position, with examples and reasons, then the second body paragraph, detailing the other side of the position, again supported by reasoning and examples, finally followed by a short conclusion.

Organization is adequate. There's a clear introduction, body, and conclusion. The language is mostly free of errors and allows comprehension. The writer displays sufficient control of language and the conventions of standard written English. However, the essay is uninspiring and not compelling at all.

Thus, for simple language, adequate organization and decent logic, a score of 4 has been assigned.

Sample Essay (Score 2)

I agreed the author, all student should studied the same syllabuses til they come into college. This is so that all students should not feel like stupid when they join becoz they are from diffrant bagrounds. Teachers also wrong to call students bad names when students dont knowed the syllabuses, so this will make the problem solved.

Also, this will help employers to make good choose who is right and wrong becoz now everyone studied same. Everyone will get same job oppochunity and not get unfair interviews.

Also, slow students will get time to pick up the knowledge. They will not get left back. This can help such people and their parents.

To conclude, the author are right in making national curriculum for all students until college.

Explanation of Score 2

The lack of good language of this essay is what most clearly earns it the score of 2. While there are spurts of clear expression, this response is hampered by grave errors in grammar and language usage, spoiling the intended meaning. It is unclear what the writer means when he/she states, "Also, this will help employers to make good choose who is right and wrong becoz now everyone studied same," or " Everyone will get same job oppochunity and not get unfair interviews."

Nevertheless, notwithstanding the numerous flaws, the writer has made an obvious attempt to respond to the prompt ("I agreed the author, all student should studied the same syllabuses til they come into college ") as well as a weak attempt to support such a stand. The flawed reasoning employed and the limited nature of the examples clearly demonstrate that the writer has not understood the statement nor considered the notion correctly enough. The whole essay response is riddled with multiple spelling errors that make the reading unpleasant and break the flow of thought [becoz, diffrant, bagrounds, knowed, oppochunity]

On the whole, the essay displays a seriously flawed but not fundamentally deficient attempt to develop and support its claims.

7.3 Essay 3 (Financial support to major cities)

Claim: Governments must ensure that their major cities receive the financial support they need in order to thrive.

Reason: It is primarily in cities that a nation's cultural traditions are preserved and generated.

Write a response in which you discuss the extent to which you agree or disagree with the claim and the reason on which that claim is based.

Understand the issue

We have to write an essay discussing whether we agree with the claim that government should financially support cities because cities preserve cultural traditions.

Discussion of the components of issue statement

The Claim

Governments must ensure – The use of the word "must" makes the suggestion of the issue quite extreme. Any sort of national suggestion should be a "should" and not a "must". This aspect should be discussed in the essay.

Their major cities – In the essay, the concept of "major" should be discussed. What makes cities "major"? Is it the total population, proportion of national population, population density, trade centre? Without setting the scope of what cities comprise "major cities", one cannot evaluate the claim correctly. Thus, essay should contain discussion on the multiple ways the term "major cities" can be interpreted and how the scenario changes the nature of the city. Another aspect that needs to be considered is that not all "major cities" in a nation will have the same nature or scope. So, how to deal with different types of "major cities" needs to be discussed in the essay.

The financial support – This implies that, according to the issue writer, cities need financial support. At this juncture, it should be worth discussing the kind of financial support that might be needed by cities and by towns and villages, and which entities deserve the financial support of the government.

In order to thrive – The financial support is meant for the cities to thrive. However, this state of "thriving" is again highly interpretative. What exactly denotes "thriving"? Is it higher standard of living, high degree of public amenities, huge volume of financial transactions, great industrial development, improved quality of life? This needs to be discussed in the essay. Another point worth mentioning is that, generally most major cities can thrive or survive without help, given the nature of development typically found in the cities. However, towns and villages may not find it easy to thrive. Should the government be directing financial support to help those thrive that cannot thrive on their own?

The reason

It is primarily in cities – This is again too extreme to claim – that something is prevalent primarily in cities. Especially, to use this kind of claim as a reason is a pointer that the claim is misdirected. The extreme nature of this portion needs to be discussed in the essay.

A nation's cultural traditions are preserved and generated – This part is completely vulnerable to criticism. The writer is claiming cities not only generate cultural traditions but also preserve them, and that is why they must be supported financially. First of all, the fact that something generates and preserves tradition is not the reason to support it financially. If it needs help to thrive that is reason to support it financially. Secondly, sociologically, most cities, because of the level of economic development in them, contain no particular brand of culture or traditions but are rather culturally indistinct because of mixing of various communities. Villages and small towns is where one would find cultural traditions being preserved, and possibly generated. This part also includes an unstated assumption that all cultural traditions are worth preserving and saving. However, till the cultural traditions are defined and evaluated, one cannot say that just because something is traditionally linked to the culture of that place, it must be preserved. Both the aspects of whether cities contain the cultural traditions and whether cultural traditions need financial support need to be discussed in the essay.

Agree because	Disagree because
Cities usually contain a big chunk of the population and should be helped if they need help	The claim and the reason may be justified as two separate things but not as a linked issue
	Cities generally don?t preserve cultural traditions; villages and small towns do
	Financial support should be given to those places that need it, not just because paces preserve tradition
	Government should help to preserve tradition, not just in major cities

Once you have thought of your position (mostly agree/mostly disagree/depends on the situation) and of some examples, start writing the essay. Don't keep brainstorming for too long in an issue task. As you write an essay, new points will come up. Incorporate them into your essay only if you can either explain them well or support them with examples.

The essay

To know best the importance of traditions, probably one needs to consult Tevye from "The Fiddler on the Roof", who explains how traditions are important in a society, especially in the context of a world changing fast. This would probably apply now more than ever. The world is on a path of accelerated growth fuelled by astonishing technology that would have seemed impossible some decades ago and spread around the globe by the internet at a pace that would have stumped all but sci-fi writers! The world is changing fast, and its cities probably faster than the rest. Given that, I mostly disagree that cities need financial support because they preserve and generate cultural traditions. In this issue, one needs to examine two concepts – on what basis should financial support be granted and who preserves cultural traditions as well as whether one should.

Before starting examination of any of the points discussed above, a fundamental point needs discussion: the definition of "major cities". The issue states that government should help major cities but fails to explain what he means when he says major cities. Depending upon whether you ask an anthropologist or an economist, the definitions of "major cities" will vary widely. Major cities could be defined by the percentage of population that resides in it, or by the density of it; it could be also defined by the amount of national income either generated or earned by it; some would define major cities as those places that are the most developed. Precisely because of the possibility of such wild variations, defining the term "major cities" is necessary.

However, for the purpose of further discourse, assuming that "major cities" are generally those places that are densely populated and economically far further than the other parts. That being established, what needs evaluating is whether these major cities preserve and generate the cultural traditions. Globalization has brought about rapid economic development in many countries, and especially so in the major cities. A side effect of the globalization has been the globalizing and homogenizing of the culture, mostly in big cities, leaving it all the same grey found worldwide in the major cities, instead of sharp, distinct vibrant colors of different cultures. Consider the case of Mumbai and New York. While the level of development may differ in these two cities, the people of Mumbai will be just as comfortable in NY, as the people would NY recognize the culture of Mumbai. A stroll in either place can yield a cup of Starbucks coffee, maybe a bite from either McDonald?s or Taco Bell, and a spot of retail therapy from Michael Kors or Nine West! Most residents of major cities are participants in the modernization phenomenon and therefore are distinct from the cultural ties of their heritage. It is more likely that one would find residents from small towns and villages still continuing with the traditions and cultures of their forefathers, much more likely than their counterparts in the cities. If we scrutinize any of numerous small towns, village and smaller cities, we would find that the people from these areas are relatively more removed from globalization and still retain the flavor of their original community and culture. Therefore, if one wants to preserve the cultural traditions, small towns, village and smaller cities and not the major cities are where one could find substantial culture to preserve.

Furthermore, one must also consider the idea that not all cultural traditions bear preserving. As the times move forward, cultures must evolve. This is most likely why Pope Francis is embracing some modern ideas, much to the horror of conservatives, and winning over those people who were neither conservatives but did not feel entirely modern either. That is not to imply that all cultural traditions are to be discarded. Culture is important because it adds a historical dimension to an individual's identity and fosters a sense of belonging. Traditions can also serve to act as a tried and tested moral compass to traverse the daily sea of activities. However, one must not blindly try to preserve anything under the term "cultural".

Finally, the issue discusses the idea of government providing financial support. The government should ensure that communities that need financial support, to thrive, to grow and to get integrated, receive the financial support. If a government decides to support any particular place only because that place preserves and generates cultural traditions, the implied message would be that modernization is unwelcome, hampering development.

To conclude, the issue discusses two valid points of providing financial support and preserving cultural traditions, but falters in linking these two independent points together. I don't disagree that government should provide financial support to any part that needs it, or that government should also work towards preserving the cultural traditions of the society. However, I do disagree with the notion that major cities preserve the cultural traditions and that they deserve financial support because of their preservation of cultural traditions.

7.4 Essay 4 (Five-year term)

> **Claim:** In any field—business, politics, education, government—those in power should step down after five years.
>
> **Reason:** The surest path to success for any enterprise is revitalization through new leadership.
>
> *Write a response in which you discuss the extent to which you agree or disagree with the claim and the reason on which that claim is based.*

Understand the issue

We have to write an essay in which we state with reasons and examples whether we agree with the claim that in all fields, the leaders should step down in 5 years because the most definite path to success is by rejuvenation brought about by new leaders.

Discussion of the components of issue statement

The Claim

In any field [business, politics, education, government] – This portion makes the issue immediately too extreme because generalizations are always generally true for any situation but not ever fully applicable in any situations. This aspect needs to be discussed in the essay that even if the claim is true, it cannot apply to all fields

Those in power – This term is pretty ambiguous. The scope of 'those in power" needs to be discussed. For example, a person may be in power but may only be a dummy leader and the true leader may be someone else, or, those in power may not be necessarily the leaders in all aspects. Does the issue imply that everyone who holds some or the other power, or some or the other leader position should step down, or does the issue mean only those who hold actual positions? Thus, this portion needs to be clarified when discussing the opinions in the issue.

Should step down – This portion too is unclear. Step down can mean either completely give up the field or take a different position. These aspects can be discussed in the essay.

After five years – This implies that all leadership talent expires in five years. This part is unclear as to whether those in power who have stepped down in five years can ever return at a later date. That aspect needs to be discussed. Further, how has the term of five years been arrived at? Do any studies show that in five years, a person will have done all he could have as far as leadership is concerned? What about the aspect of free will and democracy? What if the people want to re-elect the leader after five years? All these points should be analyzed.

The reason

The surest path – This part is again too extreme. What sort of evidence backs the "surest" path? Nothing can be sure when it comes to the complex matter of leadership. It all depends on context.

To success – The scope of the word "success" needs to be defined. Is success monetary, social, humanitarian, etc.? How can success be measured in terms of a single component? Success cannot be achieved only through leadership. Success is often the result of a group effort. Placing the entire onus of success only on leadership is taking a narrow view of a complex idea.

For any enterprise – Again, as extreme a generalization as "in any field". Nothing can hold true for "any enterprise". Each enterprise?s unique features play important parts in determining the success.

Revitalization through new leadership – Two assumptions in this portion, one that revitalization always leads to surest success, and that new leadership always brings about revitalization. What exactly does revitalization represent? Does it mean new ideas or does it mean a whole new staff and entourage? Does it mean necessarily going a different route from that of your predecessor or just going the same route differently? Thus, revitalization needs discussion in the essay. Also, "new leadership" is an ambiguous term. Is the leadership new because it is made up of young people or is it merely relatively new? Could it be that the new leadership used to be a leader in some other sphere or field and is only new to this field? The scope of newness of the leadership bears discussion.

Agree because	Disagree because
It can prevent people in power from staying too long for the sake of being powerful	Certain fields need work for a longer period, and forcing the leaders out every 5 years can leave work undone Eg.: Education reforms, civil work
Change is always constant and getting used to change is the way forward	Change for the sake of change is not necessarily right. Change should be based on correct stimulant
People can sometimes be mistaken and this mechanism can limit the harm done by bad leaders	Necessarily replacing new leaders takes the right of choice away from the people
New leadership has the potential to shake things up and prevent stagnation	New leadership for the sake of shaking things up may end up undoing the good created by the previous leaders
	Five years seems like a random number for no particular reason

Once you have thought of your position (mostly agree/mostly disagree/depends on the situation) and of some examples, start writing the essay. Don't keep brainstorming for too long in an issue task. As you write an essay, new points will come up. Incorporate them into your essay only if you can either explain them well or support them with examples.

The essay

"Change is the only constant in life", the famous quote attributed to Heraclitus seems to ring true to the issue in discussion here. While accepting change is the way to move forward, to change for change?s sake is to be too fatalistic. The issue involving whether the people in power should step down, be it from any field, every five years brings up polarizing thoughts – both for and against. However, I feel that life and its sectors are not as simplistic as this arbitrary time-based rule, and therefore, I mainly disagree with the suggestion in the issue, even though I can see some merit in it.

To first state the merits, ensuring that those in power step down every five years will make all those who have fought corruption rejoice. It is a well-known adage that "power corrupts", and leads to people who have the power much too fond of all that accompanies power. As a result, these people become unable to let go of the position, clinging on for as long as they can while doing very little of the assigned job. This random five-year rule can also prevent stagnation to quite an extent, because new leaders will always at least stir things up a bit, regardless of the merit of these stirring actions. While limiting bad leaders to a maximum damage of five years, this rule could also spur the good leaders on who know that their time is ticking away, making them anxious to finish all the good they wish to before their time is cleaved off.

Notwithstanding its considerable and tempting merits, this rule will do more harm than good because of its exceedingly general (and therefore extreme) nature and because of its arbitrary construction. First off, to suggest that this rule be applied in all fields, and possibly at all levels is too extreme a step. Not all fields are created equal and different levels need different types of treatment. For example, a school principal is far different from, say, the chief of any labour union. In the school principal's case, the changes that may be brought about in the curriculum may not be immediately noticeable, and will possibly take years to manifest. To evaluate the principal at the end of a five-year tenure, no big positives may show up. However, that would not prove that the principal has not sowed seeds of greatness to the extent he could have. Forcing him to step down and replacing him with another principal does not necessarily negate the good the earlier principal has done but it could prevent further positive from happening. On the other hand, chief of a labour-union has a lot of power, the power of the collective, backing him. Usually, the results of the extent of success of such a chief are tangible, and result-oriented. If such a person is allowed to remain in power for very long without any accountability, the person may get a negative sense of complacency and a heady sense of power, leading to unpleasant associations. In such a case, making the position result-oriented and evaluating after a set period can help keep the leader on track and from becoming too complacent. Thus, the point remains that not all leadership positions are created equal and therefore, not every field can necessarily get revitalized after a select period of time.

Furthermore, the term of five years seems rather random. In many fields, five years would be more than necessary while in others, it will be hardly sufficient, even within the same sphere at times! As an example, let's analyze two different, but leading positions within a multinational company. The leader of the sales team has clear goals and most of them achievable within a specified time-frame, possibly stretching to a year or two years at the most, if not less. On the other hand, a leader in the client-service department will have to goal of setting up a customer-friendly image for the company. It will take years for the second leader to work on the image of the company and improve it in every aspect of helping clients and customers. The results may only be evident years down the line, while there may be slow appreciation trickling in from every sector. The point is that the result period of both leaders would vary and therefore, reviewing the performance, not forcing a step down, should be done at different times for each. That brings us to the second point of the random five-year rule. The issue just suggests that every five years people should step down. A better suggestion would be that there should be periodic review for every leader after an appropriate term, not necessarily force every leader to step down after every five years, which in some cases is too many while in others is too little.

Finally, the reason for the suggestion is as extreme as the suggestion itself. To suggest that new leadership always brings about revitalization and that it is always a good thing is as extreme as saying that change is always good, without explaining for whom it is good. Sometimes, shaking up things simply to revitalize them can end up being counterproductive and can undo the good achieved up to that point. Therefore, I advise caveat emptor before buying this suggestion or its reason.

To conclude, the suggestion seems to have a good idea – to possibly keep the leaders from getting either stagnant or complacent – but fudges it up with extreme ideas. If the issue were moderated a bit, taking into account the nuanced differences of different leadership positions in different fields and the goals of those positions and toned down its recommendation from a necessary step-down to possibly a review and evaluation, the issue has some merit to it. However, its extreme wording leaves a lot to be desired and leaves me unable to agree with it .

7.5 Essay 5 (People's behavior)

> **People's behavior is largely determined by forces not of their own making.**
>
> *Write a response in which you discuss the extent to which you agree or disagree with the statement and explain your reasoning for the position you take. In developing and supporting your position, you should consider ways in which the statement might or might not hold true and explain how these considerations shape your position.*

Understand the issue

We have to write an issue essay stating whether we agree that people's behavior is controlled by factors outside their control, factors that they did not influence or make.

Discussion of the components of issue statement

People's behavior – A generalization; not very logical to try to generalize for the whole mankind. Also, the extent of the term "behavior" needs to be discussed–is it natural, instinctive behavior or premeditated, well-thought out behavior? Is it daily routine behavior or only important actions?

Largely determined – again, too extreme. This would imply that human beings are entirely thoughtless creatures, who, just as animals, merely behave as their fate would have them to. Had the issue stated "partly determined", it would be more acceptable and logical because while not everyone acts in a reactionary way, similarly, not all behave in a properly planned and controlled manner either. Most importantly, no individual can be completely characterized as either one of the two types and most people would display a combination of both types of behavior.

By forces not of their own making – this is an extremely ambiguous phrasing. This could mean something supernatural, such as fate or destiny, or it could mean just something natural but beyond a person's control, such as someone else's behavior. When discussing what affects people's behavior, such "forces" need to be specified. These forces could be surrounding, experiences, other people's influence, thoughts, analyses, etc.

Agree because	Disagree because
For many people, the environment around them provides the stimuli for their behavior	Human beings are thinking beings, capable of judging and deciding their own behavior.
Reactive behavior is quite likely dependent on forces outside a person's control	Pondered behavior will be dependent on the analyses made by the person himself.

Once you have thought of your position (mostly agree/mostly disagree/depends on the situation) and of some examples, start writing the essay. Don't keep brainstorming for too long in an issue task. As you write an essay, new points will come up. Incorporate them into your essay only if you can either explain them well or support them with examples.

The essay

An individual's behavior is the product of an array of factors, ranging from the obscure, difficult to decipher elements of the mind, to the very tangible forces of direct stimuli. So it is understandable to contend that one's behavior is largely determined by forces outside on our own control, that the peculiarities of our life's experiences, something we cannot control, have made us who we are. However it is difficult to fully agree with such a stance on human behavior, because even in the context of this multifariousness, the human mind retains the possibility of mastery over itself, and experience lends credit to the notion that though our behavior may be in part be a product of forces outside out own making, there is much we can do to shape and direct our behavior ourselves.

To start with, a resolution can be found, by asking ourselves about what drives human behavior. It is a fairly accepted notion that our behavior, the essence of who we are is influenced by our experience; right from the time we were born. We do not control where we are born, what kind of family or social environment we grew up in, or even the randomness of our own unique set of inherent abilities, but these factors all influence our outward behavior. For example, psychologists contend that children that grow up in warm, supportive homes, grow up to be more open to criticism; one can see that since the behavior of a parent is largely outside a young child's control, the effect, that is, the behavior of the child, becomes predetermined by his upbringing, and it can be thus argued that, this behavior is influenced by factors not of his or her own making. Several other example of this abound, such as the fact that children from broken homes often find it difficult to establish trust in their future relationships, or how soldiers returning from war behave and respond differently to the same situations. So in this context, it is valid to say that people's behavior is largely determined by forces outside their own making, especially if we analyze behavior that is essentially a reaction to some a set of circumstances, a default action mechanism.

Nevertheless, it is also true that enough people are acutely self-aware, and are actively involved, in their own psychological development. Because if this were not true, one could expect all of mankind to be slotted into discrete classes, all divided and neatly categorized according to the set of experiences they have had, in turn producing similar sets of behavior. However, this is far from the reality. People from the most unstable of family environments have grown to be successful, and psychologically healthy individuals, and individuals have broken free from the restraints of their own surroundings to create a different path from themselves, behavior that they have shaped, and cultivated, rather than behavior that they have passively assimilated from the random and myriad life forces outside their control. If the triumph of human mind over its sometimes rotten surroundings weren't true, rags-to-riches would never have been a catalogued phenomenon, nor would any superhero stories on overcoming childhood trauma ever be treated as inspiring!

In conclusion, human behavior may for a large part be predetermined, but such a view ignores a fundamental victory that humankind has had over randomness - the ability to control and shape their own mind, their own experiences, and break away from the predetermined nature of their own behavior. Human beings have the capacity to look at a heap of random happenings, make sense of it identify patterns, even if those patterns are in their own behavior, and some times, to make effort and successfully change their own behavior, to make it correspond not to outside factors but to their drumbeat.

7.6   Essay 6 (Free university education)

> **Governments should offer a free university education to any student who has been admitted to a university but who cannot afford the tuition.**
>
> *Write a response in which you discuss your views on the policy and explain your reasoning for the position you take. In developing and supporting your position, you should consider the possible consequences of implementing the policy and explain how these consequences shape your position.*

Understand the issue

We have to write an essay discussing whether we agree with the given suggestion that governments should pay for those students who have been accepted by universities but cannot afford the tuition.

Discussion of the components of issue statement

Governments – the *plural nature* of this word implies that the issue wishes to include the entire world in this discussion.

Should offer – this tentative phrasing clearly suggests that this is a recommendation and not an obligation. This tentativeness keeps the issue rightly mild.

Free university education – this term is too broad. "Free" as in borne by whom? The university or the government? Will any course be offered free of cost or just some specific ones?

Any student who has been admitted to a university – this too is extremely broad and general. Any university or just state ones? Will the government also fund private universities?

Who cannot afford the tuition – this is frightfully general. Who will decide affordability? How will it be determined?

Agree because	Disagree because
Education should be made available for everyone, especially anyone meritorious	Unfair to other students who get admissions. Why should some have to pay and some don't?
Providing education is the only sustainable way to reduce inequality	Can cause dependency among people and foster laziness.
Many high-quality programs are unaffordable for many students because of the high costs involved, forcing the students into debt at such an early age	Better plan would be to provide such students with loans that they can repay at a later date.
	Providing education to everyone should not be through selective benefits in this manner.

The essay

The given issue brings up strong and polarizing thoughts, best expressed by the quote "Education is the compass that one uses to navigate the vastness of life" on the one end to the quote "Give a man a fish and you feed him for a day, but teach a man to fish and you feed him for life" on the other end. There are numerous valid and strong reasons both for and against the suggestion made in the issue that governments should pay for those students who have been accepted by universities but cannot afford the tuition. However, in the interest of equity in society, agreeing with this suggestion seems difficult.

To begin with, there is no denying the noble and admirable intentions ensconced in this suggestion. To provide education to everyone deserving of it is indeed moving towards utopian ideals. Also, it is very well-established that many a worthy student is either denied the education that he deserves or he chooses not to pursue it, all due to financial constraints. These situations are dire and do merit attention and intervention.

Nevertheless, the way towards providing equitable opportunities to all does not lie in making available handouts selectively. The primary reason that begs consideration in this situation is that if such accommodations are made for students, a sense of dependency will be created and strike upon the very foundation of evolution — that is, striving and working towards greater goals. Without wishing to be sanctimonious and not wanting to turn a blind eye to the apparent problem of costly education, I wish to make the point that, making students reliant on benefits purely is actually stunting their growth. Apart from this, one should also consider that giving free education only to those who cannot afford it will generate animosity among those who can afford it. It would economically imply that those who can afford it are the ones who end up paying for their as well as others' education. Final thing to consider before providing free education is that implementation of this concept is not very practical, given that determining affordability and worthy education in a quantifiable way does not seem very possible. Additionally, today practically every country is facing mounting budget deficits, and one of the primary reasons is that the government is subsidizing far too much and not all citizens are contributing economically. There are far better ways of making sure that everyone gets equal opportunities to educate himself, if he so wishes.

Let's consider some of the possible measures that can be taken to remedy this issue. The solution that would be the easiest to implement is to provide merit-based scholarships to deserving students. Providing scholarships is different from just paying for an education because in scholarship offers, the student is held accountable for his educational progress, helping him to remain on track. Another way of making sure that education is had by all is by providing students with low-interest loans that become payable only after they have finished their education and have had sufficient time to acquire a job. Another solution that is far more long-term and will have impact on overall education society is to make education generally far more affordable and low-cost for everyone, by providing tax benefits to universities, by encouraging corporates to serve as patrons, by getting alumni to chip in to help their alma maters, etc. There can be many other innovative ways to let the student have his education while paying for it. For example, the student could be granted education by the university on the condition that he works for the university in some capacity during and after his learning until the dues are paid. Many such different solutions can be found to provide education to everyone in a just and equitable manner. To simply provide freebies can ruin the work ethic that is the bedrock of a productive culture.

To conclude, subsidizing education selectively is not the right way to provide education to everyone. However, making education available to everyone is an important benchmark of an equitable society that must be achieved. It is a probable goal that can be reached by employing a variety of tools, some of which are discussed above, and by understanding the complexity of this issue, albeit, without getting carried away by righteous-sounding but society crippling ideals .

7.7 Essay 7 (Laws should be flexible)

> **Laws should be flexible enough to take account of various circumstances, times, and places.**
>
> *Write a response in which you discuss the extent to which you agree or disagree with the statement and explain your reasoning for the position you take. In developing and supporting your position, you should consider ways in which the statement might or might not hold true and explain how these considerations shape your position.*

Understand the issue

We have to write an essay in which we state whether we agree or disagree with the statement that laws should take various aspects such as circumstances, times, and places into account.

Discussion of the components of issue statement

Laws – this word is general and encompasses all possible laws, rules and regulations. Thus the essay can discuss this from any angle.

Should be flexible enough – This is a good recommendation made towards laws and lawmakers. However, the extent of flexibility must be discussed in the essay. How flexible is enough and how much inflexibility should be maintained?

To take account of various circumstances, times, and places – This too is a good recommendation for laws. Laws should take into account various aspects. These aspects must be defined in the essay as well as possible examples of flexibility in such context should be discussed.

Agree because	Disagree because
Laws have to apply to everyone and thus should be general	Broad and general laws with no clear interpretations can be used for negative and selfish interests
Laws cannot possibly stipulate action for every possible condition that can occur and need the guidance of law for	Laws should be clear enough in their phrasing that everyone should be clear of the intent in the law
Laws cannot be misused by anyone to force only one specific measure, as opposed to multiple possible interpretations	Laws are meant to be interpreted flexibly by the executors

The essay

John Adams once passionately declared that for a society to encourage good behavior "It is more important that innocence be protected than it is that guilt be punished!" He had said so because he felt that if innocent got punished, no individual in a society would have any reason to follow the letter of the law. This quote very aptly introduces the subject at hand, the subject involving discussion on the nature of laws. Defining the exact nature of laws, whether rigid and specific or flexible and general, is very difficult, as both sides have their merits and demerits. Nevertheless, discussing merely the framing of laws without elaborating on the enforcement and upholding mechanisms of the law is meaningless.

To begin with, there are any disadvantages to rendering a rigid and inflexible wording to laws, ranging from lack of laws for special circumstances to punishing the wrong party despite extenuating conditions. For instance, if laws are too structured in their words, they would not be open to interpretation and would therefore not be applicable to multiple situations, as might have been the case were they flexible. This creates the possibility that in some situations, one may find no laws whatsoever to address the specific situation at hand! Many recent laws are examples of that, recent laws created to deal with man?s harm to environment. Had the laws been general enough all along, the action would not have been taken retrospectively. Another problem with rigidly phrased laws is that such laws do not contain the capacity to take punitive measures against the perpetrator. For example, cyber criminals often go unpunished because the justice system cannot "lawfully" establish that the alleged perpetrator had ever been in (physical) contact with the victim! If such restrictions had not been there, the interpreters of law could have easily taken the liberty to extend the law that deals with physical crimes to cover it to cyber-crimes and justice could have been served.

However, it is also true that, the very nature of rigid laws allows society to maintain law and order and seek justice. If laws were too flexible, any clever criminal could and would take advantage of it and get away with his crimes! Even when we have such rigid laws, many such cases still happen in which hard-boiled criminals have to be let off on some technicality. For example, one hears of many cases in which violent criminals had to be let go because when these criminals were arrested their Miranda rights weren?t read to them properly! Such technical details do exist for a reason, to protect the individual from the justice system?s all-too powerful stature. Even if ninety-nine guilty people are freed but one innocent is saved on the basis of these so-called loopholes, order is restored. One advantage of rigid laws is that the intent enshrined in them is clear enough to all.

All being said for and against rigid or flexible laws, it is imperative to add that laws, per se, are irrelevant in the absence of a sound judiciary system. Laws are merely frameworks but the judiciary is the platform by which laws are delivered and executed. It must be stressed that whatever faults the laws may have, either for being too rigid or for not being rigid enough, can be overcome if the interpreters of law take into account the spirit in which the laws were created. Laws by themselves would never be effective, if the people who uphold and implement the law choose for it to not be so.

To conclude, laws should tread the line between rigidity and flexibility carefully, and lawmakers should take enough care to consider all possible circumstances and cases, and build enough safeguards to ensure the innocent are never punished, even if sometimes the guilty have to be let go.

7.8   Essay 8 (Political leaders)

> **Some people believe that in order to be effective, political leaders must yield to public opinion and abandon principle for the sake of compromise. Others believe that the most essential quality of an effective leader is the ability to remain consistently committed to particular principles and objectives.**
>
> *Write a response in which you discuss which view more closely aligns with your own position and explain your reasoning for the position you take. In developing and supporting your position, you should address both of the views presented.*

Understand the issue

We have to present our views on two opposing statements. We have to state whether we agree or disagree with each of the statements and to what extent. Do we agree or disagree that political leaders must do what public says or do we believe that consistency is the main thing in any political leader?

Discussion of the components of issue statement

Some people believe – this wording creates a party with a particular opinion. We can choose to either agree with this side or disagree.

In order to be effective – whatever opinion must be of those "some people", it is with respect to "effectiveness" of a leader. This term and its implications in "leadership" can be discussed.

Political leaders must – This phrasing makes the opinion a bit extreme.

Yield to public opinion and abandon principle – Two actions are recommended – yield your own ideas and heed public's ideas. One reason cited is "to be effective".

For the sake of compromise – This is one of the main reasons cited for the two actions above. Thus, this group believes that an effective leader must give in to the public and give up his ideas only for the sake of compromise, and to be effective.

Others believe – this is introducing the opposing party to the party whose opinion we just discussed.

The most essential – the wording is again a bit extreme

Quality of an effective leader – again, "effectiveness" is at stake. It must be defined in discussing leadership.

The ability to remain consistently committed to particular principles and objectives – thus, this one does not directly negate the earlier opinion but implies so. The other party feels that to be effective a leader must be consistent. Thus, this side believes in consistency.

Agree because [agree with I and disagree with II]	Disagree because [agree with II and disagree with I]
If leaders are left to their own, they may make decisions in their interests and not necessarily beneficial to the country on the whole	People are collectively not as aware and apprised of the situation as the political leaders are and therefore letting the public decide is letting an uninformed choice happen
Forcibly sticking to a singular objective or path, even when circumstances change can be ruinous for a country?s progress	Constantly giving into the latest whims and fancies of the public will be extremely negative for the country's economy and image on the world stage
Collective intelligence is generally better than any single person's ideas	Compromise for the sake of compromise is not conducive to progress
	Consistency towards any objective yields far better returns than changing course multiple times for no reason
	Abandoning a chosen course of action merely to earn public favor is not the action of a leader; a leader is meant to lead, not follow

The essay

The given issue brings up a strong discussion point – leadership. Everyone has an idea of what leadership is and what it isn't. however, most of them can be classified into the two groups discussed in the issue – one side stating that a leader ought to heed the subjects, while the other side claiming that a leader leads and does not follow. My own ideas are very much reflected in a quote by Rosalyn Carter "A leader takes people where they want to go. A great leader takes people not necessarily where they want to go, but ought to be." While the quote may make the great leader sound extremely presumptuous, I do believe that a great leader must be prepared to make many required yet unpopular decisions.

To begin with, there is no demerit in yielding to public opinion, if the situation demands so. Many a time, the collective intellect supersedes any individual ideas and thoughts, and at such a time, the sign of a great leader would be to acknowledge that the decision demanded by the public is the superior course. However, to bow to the public for the express purpose of merely forging a compromise, so as to not endanger his own popularity, lest he may lose the next elections, is the mark of a cowardly person who ought not to have been elected at all! Compromise for the sake of compromise is just the easy, but not the right way out. If a situation arises wherein the leader must either give in to or deny the wishes of the public, then the right course does not have to be to give in. Such a situation is a true test of the leader's mettle. If the leader is convinced that the public?s wishes are detrimental to the country's progress, then he must achieve the task of convincing the public and bringing about the desired and required outcome, instead of either riding roughshod all over the people or giving in simply to avoid an unpleasant decision.

Nevertheless, a leader must always remember that he is chosen to lead the people, possibly for his visionary thinking and progressive ideas, not all of which may be considered popular. A true leader must adhere to the principals of greater good and not abandon a selected path only because the public?s opinion is turned against him at that time. Obviously, the best course of action would be to try to gain a plebiscite, but in failing to do so, the leader, after due consideration, must do what is right, and not what is popular. That is precisely the task that a leader is chosen for: to not give in to chaotic demands, to not fall prey to the vagaries and vicissitudes of time, and to not avoid the responsibility that comes with the great power bestowed on him. A great leader is expected to be aware that, despite changing times and buffeting ideas, consistency and singular dedication to any chosen objective is the most likely course to yield success. And, if the leader cannot remain disciplined towards goals set for the country, the public cannot be expected to do so either!

That being said, strong leadership should not be used to sanction autocratic measures. Just as a country should not suffer the whims of an inconstant public, nor should the country have to bear the capricious fancies of any autocrat, unjustified in his demands. Having such leaders, the public would be entirely in its right to demand new and better leaders.

To conclude, sometimes, compromise may be the need of the hour. Notwithstanding such situations, compromise for the sake of it is not preferable to maintaining a consistent course of action towards a determined course of action. That is not to say that a leader can do as he pleases in the name of leadership. Dictatorship is always displaced, sooner or later, as conveyed by "sic semper tyrannies"! Thus, leadership is not an easy mantle to bear, and even the best would falter at it. Leading people when people wish to be led can be done by any person, leader or not; only a true leader can lead people where he must, even when those people resist being led.

7.9 Essay 9 (Preservation of wilderness areas)

> **Nations should pass laws to preserve any remaining wilderness areas in their natural state, even if these areas could be developed for economic gain.**
>
> *Write a response in which you discuss your views on the policy and explain your reasoning for the position you take. In developing and supporting your position, you should consider the possible consequences of implementing the policy and explain how these consequences shape your position.*

Understand the issue

We have to write an essay on whether we agree that nations preserve any and all natural greenery in their state, regardless of its possible economic benefits.

Discussion of the components of issue statement

Nations – the scope of the essay has to be global, and not any specific locality limited.

Should pass laws – it's a recommendation, not a compulsion. The tentative phrasing makes it acceptable.

To preserve any remaining wilderness areas in their natural state – this is a bit extreme because "any" such wilderness area may not even necessarily contain vulnerable entities. What area should be protected must be defined in the essay.

Even if these areas could be developed for economic gain – while protecting the environment is important, the extreme wording is making it difficult to agree with the issue, especially since the word "wilderness" or the term "economic gain" has not been discussed. The extent of both must be discussed in the essay.

Agree because [agree with I and disagree with II]	Disagree because [agree with II and disagree with I]
Environment has been severely compromised for the sake of progress	Not all wilderness is more valuable than economic progress
If laws are not provided, individuals would not care for nature	A balanced view regarding environment and progress is better
	All green areas must be assessed and accordingly either preserved or utilized
	Not all economic activities are harmful to wilderness

The essay

The given issue statement invokes Mahatma Gandhi's apropos words "Earth provides enough to satisfy every man's need, but not every man's greed." It is indeed only now that man has begun to realize the terrible damage and its extent that the past century of progress has wreaked upon earth. Now, people are becoming aware, not nearly quickly enough, that nature is not an inexhaustible resource, but rather is an entity that needs as much care as it gives. As a result, many people are looking to preserve the earth, the environment, in a bid to undo the harm that has been done. Nevertheless, we must realize that any knee-jerk reaction to such a situation, while seemingly satisfying our offended morality, may not be the sustainable way forward.

To begin with, it is important to acknowledge that the past decades are proof that we cannot leave environment unprotected and expect it cared for, despite the obvious importance of it. To substantiate that point, one only needs to consider how long it took the global entities to act even after the alarming discovery of the hole in ozone layer was made. This bears testimony to the fact that laws are very much needed to protect and shelter the environment.

However, blindly throwing the baby out with the bathwater is not the solution. Simply banning any economic activity in anything remotely green or wild is not the sustainable way forward. The primary focus should be on sustainable development. Utopian ideals clearly demand that all harmful activities against the environment be stopped, but that is precisely why utopia is "nowhere land". As an argument against extreme measures, one must consider the Prohibition instituted by the US in the 1920s, on anything alcoholic. At that time, selling, producing or even transporting alcohol was illegal. Instead of actually curbing the use of alcohol, the Prohibition inflamed the public's desire and spawned generations of bootleggers and moonshiners! The impracticality of the whole idea was inevitably understood and the measures were withdrawn but not before leaving many much too enamored with alcohol. The lessons to be learnt from this historical episode are many, but the two fundamental ones are that extreme measures lead to extreme results and that forcing a violent change only reduces the chances of that change succeeding.

While the lessons of the Prohibition are to avoid extreme measures, they do not imply that one must not try any measures at all. Instead of merely banning all or no activities in green areas, a correct middle ground must be found. The priority, of course, must be given to the environment, given the extent of damage that needs repair. So, any wilderness that involves elements worth preserving, elements like native flora and fauna, must get protection to the maximum, to the extent that no activity, even remotely harmful be permitted in such areas. Nevertheless, not all wildernesses contains vulnerable elements, and in many such green areas, some economic activities, those that do not harm the nature, can be undertaken. For example, controlled fishery, or regulated forestry is not necessarily detrimental to the ecological balance, provided enough care is taken to not exploit it extremely. In such green areas, these innocuous economic activities can be allowed, especially if such green areas house indigenous locals who live in harmony with the nature, and those economic activities can be entrusted to those native people.

To conclude, merely ditching economic progress to save environment would not be a sustainable way forward, as ignoring people's needs to save environment would be counter-productive. Economic progress and a safe environment need not be mutually exclusive. Saving the nature needs to be an inclusive movement, and if we expect everyone to participate fully, we must make proper arrangements to not hurt the interests of such involved people, especially if those people are otherwise vulnerable. That being said, protecting the environment must be the topmost on any government's agenda, since, without ecological balance, the human race has no future, and sometimes, extreme situations may call for extreme measures.

7.10   Essay 10 (Best way to teach)

The best way to teach is to praise positive actions and ignore negative ones.

Write a response in which you discuss the extent to which you agree or disagree with the statement and explain your reasoning for the position you take. In developing and supporting your position, you should consider ways in which the statement might or might not hold true and explain how these considerations shape your position.

Understand the issue

We have to write an essay explaining whether we agree with the statement that ignoring negatives and encouraging positives is the best manner of teaching.

Discussion of the components of issue statement

The best way to teach – this wording makes the issue very extreme. This aspect must be discussed that there is no one best way; which way is the best depends on the situation.

Is to praise positive actions – this is a good suggestion. Praising positive actions lets students know when they are on the right track and lets them use it for future reference.

Ignore negative actions – this is not a very good suggestion because the students will not know when they are going wrong. Also, usually negative actions are meant to seek attention to some underlying problem. Ignoring them will not make the underlying condition go away on its own.

Agree because	Disagree because
Praising positive actions will act as positive reinforcement	There is no one best way to teach. Teaching, like any other interactive activity, requires customizing to suit the people involved
Criticism is not acceptable to everyone. Some people are more sensitive than others	Simply praising positive action while ignoring the negative ones will give any person an unbalanced view
	A person will not get any chance of improving himself, if negative actions are ignored

The essay

Teaching is one of those fundamental elements that shape the world. Like any other important issue, teaching is a subject upon which there are as many thoughts as there are teachers and pupils. The given issue brings up an important aspect of teaching: the actions of a teacher. My thoughts on the same are best summed up by a pertinent quote by one of the first philosophers of the world Zuanghzi "Rewards and punishment are the lowest forms of teaching." This is not to say that a teacher must not reward or punish their pupils, if the situation so demands, it is to say that the best way to teach involves far more than just rewards and punishment.

It is known that human beings are quite averse to change. Most change is difficult to adjust to. This aversion to change is probably from where the disinclination to learn and study stems. When a pupil is just starting out, it is likely that the pupil has been put on the path to learning, not by his own intent but by the social constructs to which he belongs. At such a time, a teacher may have his hand forced to use rewards or punishment as incentives to get the pupil to learn. In such cases, it is justified for the teacher to not only praise positive actions but also deal with negative actions of the pupil. The means of dealing with the negative actions may differ, means such as reprimands, or some such disciplining activities may be carried out, commensurate with the negative action. However, to completely ignore negative action is highly counterproductive. To begin with, if a pupil's negative actions are left ignored, then praising positive actions has no meaning per se. Praise is praise when not everything is being praised or accepted. Just as sorrow is the cutting edge by which we distinguish happiness, praise can be distinguished from the routines of life, mainly by criticism. Thus, criticism should not be avoided, if praise has to have its desirable effect. Furthermore, negative actions are mostly not negative in themselves, but rather are calls-to-action. They highlight problem areas in pupils, areas that can be remedied with attention, patience and constructive discipline. If these signs are ignored, the negative factors will take root and become habitual character traits of the pupil, especially since many a time, a pupil acts negatively through lack of awareness.

The best way to teach lies beyond positive and negative reinforcements. Teaching should not be only about rewards and punishments. The best teacher would be the one who inspires the pupils to learn, to wish to learn. The best way to teach would be to inculcate the will and intent to study and learn in the pupil, rather than make him learn through fear or enticement. However, teaching is not an absolute skill, but is a subjective practice. It has to be tailored to the pupil and his needs. Teaching, because of its very nature, cannot be a one-size-fits-all practice.

To conclude, there are many ways to teach but inconsistency should not be a part of teaching. Any effective change is brought about only by consistent practice. Thus, while the teachers should praise positive actions, to encourage the pupils in the right direction, they should not ignore the negative actions, in order to steer the pupils away from the wrong tracks. Finally, a teacher must cultivate a relationship of trust with the pupil, after which the teacher does not have to use the crude tools of reward and punishment, and can depend on the pupil's willingness to learn. The best teachers are the rudders to navigate the ocean of life.

7.11   Essay 11 (Strong and independent individuals)

> **The luxuries and conveniences of contemporary life prevent people from developing into truly strong and independent individuals.**
>
> *Write a response in which you discuss the extent to which you agree or disagree with the statement and explain your reasoning for the position you take. In developing and supporting your position, you should consider ways in which the statement might or might not hold true and explain how these considerations shape your position.*

Understand the issue

We have to write an essay explaining whether we agree that luxury and conveniences keep people from becoming stronger and more independent, and we must provide reasons and examples for our beliefs.

Discussion of the components of issue statement

The luxuries and conveniences – what exactly constitutes these can be discussed or a general view of them can be taken.

Of contemporary life – this issue is speaking exclusively about modern life. In such a case, luxuries and conveniences can be defined as those that have been around in recent times.

Prevent people from developing – this part implies that because earlier people did not have luxuries and conveniences, they were necessarily stronger and more independent and that none of them were not so!

Into strong and independent individuals – the connection between luxuries, conveniences and strength, independence must be discussed. How exactly are these things related?

Agree because	Disagree because
Struggle forces people to adapt and innovate	An individual's own mind plays a role in determining strength and independence
Luxuries and conveniences, if had from the beginning reduce the desire to improve	Independence and strength does not have to be mutually exclusive to conveniences and luxuries
	Luxuries and conveniences free a person's time to allow for higher challenges

The essay

The issue topic seems to bring up lot of pop culture and its accompanying mainstream criticism and hipster praise, but it actually brings up quite a valid point of discussion – whether the luxuries and conveniences of the modern life are making us weaker and dependent. This connection is not unique. The same allusions have been made regarding many recent developments, such as the internet, computers, etc. The same issues are raised regarding the effects of those modern developments too. Nevertheless, when it comes to anything related to human beings, nothing is simplistic or that black-and-white. Each side has its merits and demerits and there's no clear resolution.

To begin with, there is quite a lot of merit in the argument against luxuries and conveniences and for struggle. It is said that struggle builds character and teaches a person the value of things. Struggle for existence is the very basis of evolution, evolution that brought us human beings to this point of absolute independence on earth! Had there been no struggle, there probably would not have been human beings exerting free will all over the planet. Also, struggling for things makes us aware of the value of things that we are struggling for. It makes us appreciate those things far more than we otherwise would have. We all can see that ready availability of resources such as fossil fuels has brought us to this point that we are carelessly overusing them, even to the detriment of the whole planet. On a philosophical level too, people who struggle and who don't have luxuries and conveniences of an easy, wealthy life grow up to become sensitive but strong and independent yet compassionate people. The history of the world is full of such examples: Genghis Khan, Alexander the Great, Pele, JK Rowling, Sylvester Stallone! Adversity does have the tendency to sharpen and hone people's best qualities.

That being said, it is not fair to suggest that anyone who has had luxuries and conveniences will not be a strong or independent person. Such qualities are not mutually exclusive to physical comforts. In fact, strength and independence have more to do with a person's character than his social standing. There have been numerous people who were born into wealth and luxury, despite which they chose to become strong, independent thinkers by themselves. For instance, Gautam Buddha was born a prince, in the lap of luxury, but that did not stop him from pursuing, with incredible strength and independence, his own chosen path. Another such example is Bertrand Russell, who despite being titled and wealthy, surrounded by luxuries, did not forfeit humanity or humility and carved out his position in the world with supreme intelligence and strength.

To conclude, strength and independence do no exclusively lie within the domains of struggle and inconveniences. While lack of luxuries and of conveniences can spur a person on to struggle and reach for greater levels, the presence of such luxuries and conveniences will not stop the determined individuals from pursuing what they wished to, from being strong and independent in their character. There are just as many examples suggesting that luxuries spoil a person, as there are those suggesting that they allow a person greater latitude in seeking out greater things. Implying that luxuries and conveniences directly affect a person's development, or lack thereof, is taking a myopic view, especially given the superb things human mind and human beings are capable of.

7.12   Essay 12 (Indicator of a great nation)

> **The surest indicator of a great nation is represented not by the achievements of its rulers, artists, or scientists, but by the general welfare of its people.**
>
> *Write a response in which you discuss the extent to which you agree or disagree with the statement and explain your reasoning for the position you take. In developing and supporting your position, you should consider ways in which the statement might or might not hold true and explain how these considerations shape your position.*

Understand the issue

The issue statement claims that the level of general welfare of people in the nation decides the greatness of that nation, and not the achievements of its rulers, artists or scientists.

Discussion of the components of issue statement

The surest indicator – this wording makes the issue very extreme sounding. This wording should be toned down a bit to make it more acceptable. The extreme nature of this wording must be discussed. Also "indicator" makes it sound like there is just one possible indicator.

Of a great nation – greatness is a subjective concept, and not a quantifiable, tangible notion. How greatness is measured needs to be discussed.

Is represented – One needs to discuss the fact that since a nation is made up of all kinds of individuals, so would greatness, welfare, etc would differ by that many definitions. It cannot be pinned down specifically to black-and-white.

Not by the achievements of its rulers, artists, or scientists – this wording makes it sound like the two concepts are mutually exclusive, but they don't have to be.

But by the general welfare of its people – welfare of people is important but so are achievements of artists and scientists. Why can't a nation focus on both?

Agree because	Disagree because
Nations should focus on greater good and not on the select few	The two things are not mutually exclusive; a nation can have both achievements of artists and scientists and high level of general welfare of its people
Overall greater level of welfare of people will automatically improve the chances of its artists and scientists too	Improvements in life and in entertainment are generally brought about by artists and scientists and their contribution to the world; it is important to nurture their talents specially
A nation's first duty is towards improving the overall community	

The essay

Generalizations always fail to take into account the specifics and miss the big picture, as does the given issue statement. While the statement brings to bear a very valid discussion, the greatness of a nation, it does so in extreme terms, terms with which agreeing is unreasonable. While one can say that the level of general welfare of its people determines the greatness of a nation, it must not be at the expense of the achievements of its rulers, artists or scientists.

Primarily, since all different types make up a nation, a nation must look after its entire people, including elite and not just the general populace. To suggest that one must not focus on the achievements of its artists or scientists is to imply that these people are not important, when compared to the rest of the population. A nation does not have to choose between the two, since there's no need for it to be an either-or situation. A nation, a great one, can look after the general welfare of its population just as much as it can nurture the artists and scientists.

Furthermore, greatness is a subjective concept. If a nation chooses to focus only on its artists and scientists, things can go severely awry, as Russia did. Focussing on a select portion of the population can generate a lot of resentment among the others, and can put tremendous pressure on the chosen selective few. Russia's grooming of its talented people had such a mixed bag of results. Russia had some of the best scientists and writers, painters and dancers, in that time but very few of them actually wanted to remain in Russia! Even the rest of the population was either desperately trying to be the selective few or trying to not be part of the population at all.

On the other hand, when a nation focuses too much on the general welfare of its citizens, the collective character of the nation tends to slide, with people becoming excessively dependent on the welfare state and becoming unproductive. For instance, UK is facing such a crunch in a rather extreme manner. UK has overdone the welfare state part, resulting in a nation full of people, reluctant to work, and those who are just an unproductive burden on the state. This has possibly led to the effect that UK faces a major problem trying to curb down people who cheat the government for benefits.

UK's citizens are happy, and people from other nations want to come to UK too, causing tense situations.

To conclude, if a nation has to be great, it has to straddle the line between supporting its population to grow and evolve and helping to nurture its artists and scientists. A nation's greatness is subjective and cannot be broken down into a simple this or that; it must be complex and ever-adapting. To say that the surest indicator of the nation's greatness is the general welfare of its people is to take a narrow view to the issue. A great nation is the one that strives towards greatness by helping both the general population and the artists and scientists.

7.13   Essay 13 (Teachers' salaries)

> **Teachers' salaries should be based on their students' academic performance.**
>
> *Write a response in which you discuss the extent to which you agree or disagree with the claim. In developing and supporting your position, be sure to address the most compelling reasons and/or examples that could be used to challenge your position.*

Understand the issue

We need to write an essay discussing whether teacher's salaries should be linked to their students' academic performance.

Discussion of the components of issue statement

Teachers' salaries – This component introduces that all professional teachers should have performance linked salaries.

Should be based on – This part simply introduces that the two things must be linked. To what extent or how much has not been discussed at all. The impossibility of the logistics of such a maneuver should be discussed.

Their students' academic performance – This part explains that teachers should get paid as per the academic performance of their students. Thus, this issue is applicable only to academic teaching. Also, this part suggests that the best proof of learning is the academic performance of a student. Also, there are numerous factors that affect a student's academic performance, such as curriculum, exam patterns, school and home environment, textbook, aptitude etc. To link teachers' salaries to student's performance is unfair.

Agree because	Disagree because
Some subjects are performance oriented, such as math, computer coding, etc.	Academic performance is not an indicator of how much students learned
Incentivizing performance can improve performance, in general	Exams don't accurately judge a student's overall progress in any particular subject
	Student's academic performance is influenced by many factors such as textbook, aptitude, environment, etc
	Some subjects cannot improve over just a period of time, it takes longer to improve —languages
	Judging progress in certain subjects is impossible - physics, biology, etc.

The essay

Before beginning a discussion on the topic given in the issue, a quote from Plutarch is worth mentioning "the mind is not a vessel to be filled, but a fire to be kindled." The issue presents a suggestion that teachers' salaries be linked to their students' performance. To evaluate this suggestion, one must consider various aspects, feasibility of this maneuver, possible responses from the teachers, but primarily the purpose of education.

To begin with, the issue statement is probably a valid reaction generated out of concern for the quality of education that students receive and whether the learning remains long-term and benefits the learners. Some alarming trends have been noticed, trends such as students' lack of math skills, improper communication abilities, etc. Addressing such concerns should be top priority to ensure that students get proper education. Among possible measures, one measure can be linking performance of students to teachers' salaries, performance in quantifiable areas, such as math, computer, etc.

Nevertheless, merely linking teachers' remuneration to students' performance, apart from being unviable logistically, is a bad idea; it is putting the cart before the horse. The goal of education is not to ensure quantitative retention of concepts and subjects but to facilitate qualitative assimilation of ideas and notions. As it is, one can see that education systems suffer from exam – or scoring– oriented teaching, affecting the quality of learning. A move, the kind suggested by the issue, would exacerbate the situation. It will incentivize those teachers who can get their students to score the maximum on the exams, thereby reducing the importance given to overall learning, especially in subjects such as the sciences, arts, humanities, languages, etc. While performances may see an improvement, the students may not be any better off than they were before.

To improve the quality of education and learning one needs to address the whole picture. Simply reinforcing academic performance will not achieve the desirable results. The problems are numerous, ranging from inadequate and invalid examination patterns to insipid, mechanized curricula. So, steps must be taken to infuse life into the curricula of the various subjects, making those subjects interesting and worth studying. The curricula should include actual demonstrations of concepts, instead of mere book learning, should incorporate live assignments, should explain tangibly to the extent possible and generally be made as interesting as it can be. Also, examination and grading systems should be worked upon to come as close to judging learning and understanding rather than judging rote learning. Rote learning has its merits only in certain fields, and should be accordingly encouraged. However, in most subjects, understanding the fundamentals and the ideas that spring from those basics is the learning required. Examinations can be altered to judge more of such learning, perhaps by more practice-centered assignments, field-work, subjective tests, etc.

To conclude, linking teachers' salaries to students' performance has many pitfalls. One of them is the difficulty in actually executing this move: how much of the salary must be linked to performance, what would be considered a good performance, will students' feedback be taken into account, etc. Besides the sheer impossibility of the physical mechanics of such a move is the bigger problem of ignoring the underlying cause of all troubles – insufficiency of the education system. Simply providing a cosmetic solution, such as the one suggested in the issue may make the symptoms disappear but will not cure the problem.

7.14   Essay 14 (Greatness of individuals)

> **The greatness of individuals can be decided only by those who live after them, not by their contemporaries.**
>
> *Write a response in which you discuss the extent to which you agree or disagree with the statement and explain your reasoning for the position you take. In developing and supporting your position, you should consider ways in which the statement might or might not hold true and explain how these considerations shape your position.*

Understand the issue

The issue claims that only those people who come after, the later generations, can decide the greatness of individuals of earlier generations, and that the people of the same time cannot decide the greatness. We have to write an essay discussing this issue and whether we agree with it, and to what extent.

Discussion of the components of issue statement

The greatness of individuals – This wording introduces an ambiguous phrase "greatness". While many definitions can be discussed for it, one can also discuss greatness as genius and discuss the issue from that point of view. Greatness can be discussed as genius, talent, merit, etc.

Can be decided – Decided is an unclear term. What exactly does it entail? One can discuss this aspect as fame, recognition, awards, etc. or it can be discussed as some other form of validation.

Only by those who live after them – The word "only" makes this issue too extreme. To suggest that only the subsequent generations can decide the greatness is incorrect. There are cases for and against both sides. This extreme nature should be evaluated in the essay.

Not by their contemporaries – There are too many examples contradicting this viewpoint, such as Newton, Galileo, Einstein, Beatles, Picasso, Da Vinci, etc. to completely agree with this issue. Equally, there are many examples for this point too to completely disagree with it. A balanced approach is best, discussing both sides and explaining that no one side is necessarily applicable.

Agree because	Disagree because
Great people's ideas often are beyond the current time frames E.g. – Vincent Van Gogh	Many great people have gotten recognized in their time, as much as later E.g. – Einstein, Mahatma Gandhi
Many times the ideas can be evaluated or come into play at a much later date E.g. – Gregor Mendel	Greatness of many individuals is contextual, and people who don't belong to that context may not understand, especially in the case of music artists who become famous in their time and are either ignored or ridiculed by later generations

The essay

The issue brings to mind the words of Ralph Waldo Emerson "Greatness is a property for which no man can receive credit too soon; it must be possessed long before it is acknowledged." Along the same lines, it is quite believable to say that the greatness of individuals is decided by the subsequent generations, rather than by the contemporaries. However, it is incorrect to suggest that only the subsequent generations can do so, and that the contemporaries will never be able to determine greatness; there are examples aplenty for both sides.

To begin with, many geniuses were appreciated within their time as much as subsequently. For instance, while Einstein's greatness or genius is ever more appreciated as time goes by, despite multiple challenges to his theories, people of his time too accepted Einstein as a genius, even if they could not have comprehended the extent of it. So too was the case for such famous people as Galileo, Newton, Niels Bohr, the Beatles, Picasso, etc. They achieved recognition and respect as much among their contemporaries as they did posthumously. One can argue that the contemporaries possibly could not imagine the extent of the greatness and genius of those great people, in that time, given the limitations of art, science and culture of that time. That would indeed be true. Nonetheless, they did not let those great luminaries languish without acknowledgment. Therefore, it would be incorrect to suggest that greatness can only be decided by the later generations and not by the contemporaries. This statement is not necessarily true without exceptions.

On the other hand, history is replete with examples of people, geniuses and greats, who died without knowing how much they were applauded by the world for their work and greatness, regrettably after their deaths. The best example that comes to mind is full of poignant, bittersweet aspects, that of Vincent Van Gogh. Today, Van Gogh is revered for his post-Impressionist style, dripping with emotion, movement and vibrancy. In fact, his work, considered among the most valuable, sells for record-breaking, unprecedented sums: his Portrait of Dr. Gachet sold for $82.5 million in 1990, making it one of the most expensive paintings ever sold! Most unfortunately though, in his own time, Van Gogh was treated as a failure, a laughingstock. Even though he produced more than 2000 pieces of art, he sold only 2 during his short, unhappy life. Suffering with mental illness and further depressed by his lack of success, Van Gogh committed suicide at the age of 37. Rebuked when he was alive, Van Gogh was considered highly influential subsequently, inspiring generations of artists, and has the most respected and regarded paintings in modern art. Now, so was a genius who was completely unappreciated in his own time, but whose greatness was accurately measured and accorded by subsequent generations. Thus, it does happen that an individual's greatness is not accurately evaluated or determined by his peers by is by the later generations.

Moreover, sometimes, contemporaries of great individuals cannot measure the greatness of the geniuses because the geniuses are far ahead of their times, given their visionary thinking. Such a discrepancy leaves the peers incapable of determining the greatness of an individual. One such case was of Gregor Johann Mendel, who we now know as the Father of Modern Genetics because he established Mendelian rules of inheritance. In his own life, having multiple financial difficulties, he became a Friar but pursued scientific inquiries. In his extensive experimental garden, Mendel patiently spent seven years of his life breeding and cross-breeding peas, carefully documented his work and developed what would eventually be known as Mendel's Laws of Inheritance. While his work got published in one of the lesser-known journals of that time, the greatest minds of his time couldn't understand him. It wasn't until 16 years after his death that three independent botanists rediscovered Mendel's work, eventually proving all of Mendel's work, thereby establishing him a genius, albeit posthumously. So it is that many a time, an individual's peers are too limited in their thinking and the individual is so far ahead in his thinking that the greatness of the individual remains undetermined by his peers, and only the people of the following generations can truly gauge the greatness of such a mind.

To conclude, it is incorrect to suggest that all great individuals have been not accorded their dues by their own peers. The many examples for and against this claim leave the entire issue far too complex and subjective to have a clear winning side.

7.15   Essay 15 (Saving endangered species)

> **Society should make efforts to save endangered species only if the potential extinction of those species is the result of human activities.**
>
> *Write a response in which you discuss your views on the policy and explain your reasoning for the position you take. In developing and supporting your position, you should consider the possible consequences of implementing the policy and explain how these consequences shape your position.*

Understand the issue

We have to write an essay discussing whether we agree with the statement that endangered animals should be attempted to be saved by the society only if the danger to those animals has been posed by human activities.

Discussion of the components of issue statement

Society should make efforts – This issue seems to be addressed to everyone in general. Generalizations always tend to be extreme. Stakeholders within society can be discussed, such as corporates, communities, individuals, etc.

To save endangered species – this issue is restricting itself only to endangered species. It is not discussing any proactive measures, merely trying to recommend some corrective action of saving those species that are endangered. This aspect, lack of prevention, can be discussed.

Only if the potential extinction of those species – The word "only" makes this issue too extreme. It implies extreme action. Why should we save only some species from extinction?

Is the result of human activities – The suggestion that we should save only those species that we have put in danger brings up two aspects. One — whether it is possible to accurately assess and pin down all possible harm, direct and indirect, that human activities have caused, to accurately judge which species is endangered because of human activities? Two - whether, as human beings and dominant species, we have no responsibility to save any species that we can regardless of whether we endangered it?

Agree because	Disagree because
Sometimes, animals are in danger of extinction because they are unfit to survive the changing	All species are important and usually have some ecological niche, and letting them go extinct can cause ecological damage.
Human beings are the dominant species and have the capability to protect other species, and so they ought to	It is impossible to assess the extent of human impact, and whether a particular species was endangered because of human activities and to what extent.

The essay

Before beginning the discussion on the issue statement, a pertinent quote by Voltaire bears mentioning "With great power comes great responsibility". The issue statement suggests that people should make an effort to save only those species that are endangered as a result of human activities. This issue opens up the discussion with two aspects in scope: damage caused by human activities, and the responsibility of saving endangered species. While human beings do not have the power to save all species from becoming extinct, some faster than others, to say that we only save those that we harmed is an extremely callous position to adopt.

To begin with, it can be conceded that we truly cannot even begin to save all species on the brink of extinction, many of which are becoming extinct faster than we can even realize their presence. Nature will have its way. And, many times, species will go extinct, help or no help, because its individuals could not adapt to the changing circumstances or could not be helped by human beings. For example, even when human beings try to improve the conditions for some severely threatened species, say by creating biosphere reserves, not all species are able to breed in captivity, thereby suffering from dangerously low numbers overall, and a terrifyingly shrinking gene pool. Those are such species that probably will be lost to the world forever.

Nevertheless, there are many species that we can help, and substantially too. At this juncture, to decide that we should try to save only those that were endangered by human activities is to not realize the great responsibility that we owe given the great power human beings have, as the dominant species, over the rest of the natural world. First of all, even if we try to ascertain which species we have endangered, we may not be able to, because we are not a discrete piece but an inseparable part of nature. It is impossible to pin down, the innumerable ways we have had an impact within the ecology of the earth. Having formed large communities and given ourselves industries and technology, we have gone to great lengths and usurped most of the natural resources available, eventually threatening our own survival, let alone that of any other species! Given such history, suggesting that we save only select species is preposterous because we wouldn't begin to know how many species we have, inadvertently or otherwise, affected. Thus, since we cannot quantify the extent of damage caused by human activities we should not withhold help from those species that we can. Furthermore, given that we seem to be the only creatures granted the ability to reason, we have an ethical responsibility, as we, unlike any other species, can gauge when any species is in danger. To withhold our help is downright mean and unjust.

To conclude, human beings have caused unquantifiable, and often irreversible, damage to the environment, causing the domino effect affecting species all over. This change puts the responsibility of undoing the damage and saving affected species squarely on our shoulders. Instead of apportioning blame and trying to wriggle out of our dues, we must step up and do what must be done.

7.16   Essay 16 (Means taken to attain goal)

> **If a goal is worthy, then any means taken to attain it are justifiable.**
>
> *Write a response in which you discuss the extent to which you agree or disagree with the statement and explain your reasoning for the position you take. In developing and supporting your position, you should consider ways in which the statement might or might not hold true and explain how these considerations shape your position.*

Understand the issue

We have to write an essay discussing whether we agree that any and all means to attain a worthy goal are justifiable.

Discussion of the components of issue statement

If a goal is worthy – This issue aspect discusses goals and worthiness, but does not define either. Without discussing the scope of these words, the issue is ambiguous. Also, who should be the final authority in determining worthy goals?

Then any means taken – this wording is very extreme. Any means can entail dangerous, illicit, unethical, unfair, unjust, violent activities. The acceptable means need to be discussed. In fact, this is a very extreme suggestion. Not all means are acceptable.

To attain it are justifiable – This issue suggests that if any person decides that a particular goal is worthy, he or she may use any measures to attain the goal, without any worrying about the consequences. This is extremely incorrect in the context of human society.

Agree because	Disagree because
Sometimes, the only way to ensure that the right thing gets done is to use whatever means are at one's disposal, regardless of consequences	Worthiness of a goal is a subjective notion, not an objective, clearly idea
	A means of doing things that is acceptable to someone may not always be in the best interests of another person
	Such a claim can be used in many illegal, unfair and unjust
	This can be the start of the end for the human society

The essay

This issue essay strongly reflects Niccolo Machiavelli's words "the ends justify the means", bringing up an ongoing debate in the field of ethics and morality. While the words of this issue statement seem full of verve and vigor, worthy of inspiring extreme fervor and passion, a careful evaluation of the deeper implications of the words will reveal that the layers bear the potential to create anarchy and dissent.

It is understandable that sometimes the only way to achieve certain goals is to seize any chance that presents itself. This is especially true in case of any oppressed nation. History is replete with stories of how nations and masses made themselves independent of the moneyed classes by throwing off the shackles of various forms of oligarchies. At such times, many heinous acts, acts that would shame humanity, were committed. For instance, the French Revolution was at the cost of Louis XVI and Marie Antoinette, among countless others. While freedom was an inalienable right of the French people, executing powerless and enfeebled monarchs was symbolic yet unnecessary. All such revolutions bear the heavy price of bloodshed. Even though the ends seem noble and necessary, thereby rationalizing the means, they aren't always so.

Primarily, to suggest that any means whatsoever are justifiable to attain a so-called worthy goal is to imply that as long as someone deems something worthy, he can get away with anything! Who would be the arbiter of what's worthy and therefore what means are justified? Additionally, the issue seems to not address the very relevant point of consequences. That the use of any means to attain some worthy goals will have repercussions goes without saying. Apart from lack of clarity as to which entity bears the right to determine worthiness of goals and justifiability of the means employed, another question that plagues us is the apportioning of due responsibility of consequences and repercussions. When people start snatching worthy goals using any means, who would be watchdog to ensure that no innocent party gets hurt in that process? Also, even if some such mishap occurs, who would initiate and enforce corrective measures? A just society, an equitable society is always identified by the way it protects its vulnerable elements. Finally, such a belief that ends justify the means may encourage socially disruptive behavior, putting at risk the foundations of a peaceful community. The fabric of human society will be rent apart! This would encourage the words "Might is right"!

To conclude, there are justifiable situations in which using any means available is to attain a worthy goal is imperative. However, one must be careful about defining such goals. Those goals that benefit the maximum sections, not catering to selfish or vested interests, can often be pronounced worthy. Equally, any goal that marginalizes the weaker levels of society is not likely to be a rational, justifiable one. Exercising caution with regard to the means and measures is also important. One cannot reasonably agree that any means, provided that the goals are worthy, is justifiable. Not all means are acceptable. Means that don't harm others in pursuit of necessary and worthy goals can be considered justifiable and defendable. Thus, while some situations may demand extreme measures, one cannot sweepingly concur with the statement that worthy goals deserve completion through any possible means.

7.17 Essay 17 (Increasingly rapid pace of life)

> **The today causes more problems than it solves.**
>
> *Write a response in which you discuss the extent to which you agree or disagree with the statement and explain your reasoning for the position you take. In developing and supporting your position, you should consider ways in which the statement might or might not hold true and explain how these considerations shape your position.*

Understand the issue

We have to write an essay discussing whether we agree that our fast-paced lives causes more trouble than saving us trouble.

Discussion of the components of issue statement

The increasingly rapid pace of life – The main point of discussion seems to be that the pace of life has increased and is continuing to increase, and this increasing pace is a problem. Thus, we can discuss examples denoting increased pace of life.

Today causes – increased pace of life is being held responsible for certain things. We should discuss the extent to which the increased pace of life is responsible for things, and also discuss what other things may be causing the problems being linked with increased pace of life.

More problems than it solves – The issue does not explain the word "problems". We need to define the scope of that word and explain how whether pace of life is responsible for those problems. Examples of such instances can be used.

Agree because	Disagree because
People are losing touch with basic skills	The pace of life is not responsible for the major problems we face today.
E.g.: Math and calculations, communication, etc.	E.g.: Global warming is not caused by the pace of life but by incorrect and unmeasured use of resources
People who can't cope up; may get left behind, in their jobs, life, school, etc.	To improve basic systems of our lives is a basic characteristic of human thinking
	Increased pace allows us to spend more time on other things
	Increased pace also challenges us to become faster and adapt

The essay

Change has often been debated, from the beginning of times. Thomas Hardy verily exclaimed "Time changes everything except something within us that is always surprised by change." This quote seems highly relevant to the discussion brought forth by the issue at hand, the increasing pace of life and its part in creating problems or solving them. Like all generalizations of complex ideas, this generalization too seems applicable to everything in general but nothing in specific. It is indeed very comforting to attribute the majority of the problems of the modern world to the handiest candidate available – change, or specifically in this case, the increasing pace of life. After all, the increasing pace of life is forcing us to adapt or find ourselves left behind, in our jobs, schools, very lives. The increasing pace of life, brought about by technology, can also be blamed for our losing touch with many basic skills that were otherwise taken for granted. For instances, use of calculators can be blamed for declining math skills of students, or increased dependence on communication gadgets can be blamed for lack of communication skills.

However, actually blaming calculators and gadgets is the equivalent of implying that use of foot scales is the reason humans cannot draw straight lines with their hands, or that using pressure cooker to speed up the cooking process creates more problems than it solves! Like all change, the increasing pace of life today brings its challenges. One does need to get used to constantly changing technology, advances in other aspects of living, etc. Despite these challenges, life is on the whole better. For instance, time to travel or communicate has reduced drastically from what it used to be, say, even just two decades ago. However, faster travel or communication has solved far more problems than it has created. Same is true for faster processing in the computers, faster industrial processes, faster medical procedures, laparoscopy and the likes, quicker learning or training methods, etc. all such advances have solved a multitude of problems, saved countless man-hours and improved the quality of human life immeasurably. Such changes always bring the danger of obscuring the skills one may have worked hard to acquire. For example, an expert stenographer, or a calligraphist, may find himself with a frightening turn of events, a world in which neither stenography nor calligraphy seems necessary. In such a scenario, the only way forward is through adapting to the changed status quo, perhaps either by learning a new skill or by using the original skill in a novel way. Necessity is the mother of invention after all. Nonetheless, to blame change, in this case, rapid pace of life, for such unfortunate but inevitable situation, is not quite right.

On the other hand, all change brings with itself a period of turbulence. The same can be said for the increasingly rapid pace of life too. Since the society is not used to dealing with the rapid changes, proper protocol to incorporate these changes and move with them has not been formed yet. That is why we find that while technology saves humans amazing amount of time, the humans seem to fritter away most of that saved time on innocuous things. What needs to be done is set appropriate higher challenges to optimize the positives of the rapid pace of life. As a crude example, as a calculator allows a child to finish calculation work faster than before, the child should be given more complex problems to ensure that the time saved by the calculator is used to develop the child faster, enabling him to improve faster rather than languish with the extra time available. Such a change is noticed in TV viewing trends already. It was found that people's attention started drifting very easily, given the numerous distractions available in today's rapid culture. So, if a camera lingered too long, people's minds would wander and ultimately lose interest in the program before them. The TV programmers rose to the challenge and devised just as slow but extremely engaging content, eventually bringing about what is famously called the golden age of TV series, with widely acclaimed shows such as Dexter, Breaking Bad, House of Cards, Game of Thrones, etc. to name just a few. Thus, the increased pace has stimulated and brought about better change.

To conclude, change is a constant, and the rapid pace of life is a change in process. One may moan about it to temporarily feel better, but one will have to get used to it, or be left behind. The society should devise the next levels of adaptations to ensure that the rapid pace of life does not end up harming the next generations by creating too much leisure that allows deadening of minds, but creates higher set of challenges to utilize the time saved for better pursuits. Also, the rapid pace of life should not prevent us from pursuing peace, calm, and ultimately contentment in this buzzing, frenetic world.

7.18   Essay 18 (Regarding any living human as a hero)

Claim: It is no longer possible for a society to regard any living man or woman as a hero.

Reason: The reputation of anyone who is subjected to media scrutiny will eventually be diminished.

Write a response in which you discuss the extent to which you agree or disagree with the claim and the reason on which that claim is based.

Understand the issue

A claim has been made and a reason has been given. The issue states that because the intense media scrutiny affects everyone's reputation, it is not possible to for a society to have any heroes. We have to write an essay discussing whether we agree with that claim and the reason on which the claim is dependent.

Discussion of the components of issue statement

The claim part:

It is no longer possible for a society – The issue deals with society's perceptions on the whole, not from an individual or any other point of view. Thus, the issue must be addressed from the community's viewpoint, or even global or national frame of reference.

To regard any living man or woman as a hero – the issue curiously restricts itself to "living" men or women, thereby suggesting that dead or long-gone people can be regarded by societies as heroes. This issue implies that to be regarded as a hero by a society, one has to be dead.

The reason part:

The reputation of anyone – The word "reputation" brings perception into scope. Thus, the issue does not state that actual character of a person will make it impossible for a person to be regarded as a hero, but rather that his reputation will make it difficult. This aspect can be discussed in the issue, with examples.

Who is subjected to media scrutiny – This part implies that all heroes are subjected to media scrutiny, which is true mostly. Also, the media scrutiny has been used to denote that if someone is constantly evaluated, sooner or later some negative aspect of that person will come to public notice.

Will eventually be diminished – This part suggests that all heroes fall, and that societies demand a lot from its heroes. With time, always something will happen, causing the heroes to fall.

Agree because	Disagree because
In today's times, almost every idolized person eventually loses the respect of society	Society's perceptions about "heroism" are changing. Heroes are no longer unreal, impossible super-humans but average individuals.
E.g.– Tiger Woods, Lance Armstrong, etc.	E.g. – Edward Snowden, Julian Assange, Malala Yousafzai
Media scrutiny today is extreme and intense, bearing down not just on famous but also on ordinary people	This is not true just for living man or woman. This also happens to people long dead.
	It is incorrect to blame the media for the faults of the people deemed as heroes. The media is merely doing its job, investigating.

The essay

Heroism is a subjective concept, changing from individual to individual. Society has some stock definitions for what it deems heroic. Society usually perceives selfless do-gooders as heroes. Also those people who battle enormous odds to attain an important goal, generally bigger than just a selfish goal, are also considered heroes. History abounds with such examples. People who die serving others, such as Nathan Hale or countless other revolutionaries are heroes, and so are people who lived their lives helping others in need, such as Mother Teresa or Florence Nightingale. The given issue statement seems to make a very uncanny but debatable claim that in today's times, it is impossible for a society to have heroes, not for long. Media scrutiny will eventually fell such heroes. While there are many examples to support this claim, and the underlying reason, there are many examples against it too, supported mainly by society's changing perceptions on heroism.

On the one hand, numerous examples spring ready to support the point that whenever heroes are built in today's world, the continuous glare of media's scrutiny eventually topples those heroes. For instance, Tiger Woods, Lance Armstrong, Michael Jackson prove the point "The bigger they are, the harder they fall". Each of those was at the top of his field; the trendsetter, the icon in his area for a long period before eventually having a massive and public fall from grace. One can argue that if they had not been under media's eye, their activities would not have come to attention, leaving their fame intact. However, even then, they still would have committed the wrong, unethical things that they did, making them undeserving of the respect heaped upon them by the public. Thus, while it seems true that these living heroes fell, to suggest that they did so because of media scrutiny is incorrect. With or without media scrutiny, the wrong actions of those people remain, and without media attention, it would have gone unpunished.

On the other hand, the issue restricts itself to living people, and claims that only living people are subjected to media scrutiny, making it impossible for a society to have heroes. However, that is not true, because media scrutiny often extends to people long gone too. Many a time, a person long dead has been dragged through the mud by the media when that person's allegedly incorrect activities have come to fore, as such things often do when classified information is declassified. One such example is that of Martin Luther King who was, quite shockingly, accused, after his death, of having been adulterous. It shook the faith of many in the man. Another primary point against the issue is society's changing notions and perceptions about heroism. No longer are only extraordinary, rare people being deemed heroic. The society is moving towards a new idea of heroism, in which special qualities in ordinary, average people being considered superb and heroic. For example, Malala Yousafzai is the youngest ever Nobel laureate, celebrated for her brave resistance to terrorist and unprogressive elements that wanted to prevent education of girls. People like Edward Snowden and Julian Assange are also regarded as icons, advancing the cause of free speech and keeping the governments from getting too big. These icons haven't been tumbled yet. Even if some terrible secret of theirs comes out in the open, the society is becoming more and more progressive in its outlook, and realizes that while these people have done some great things, they are human and subject to human frailties. Thus, these changing perceptions may yet grant us some heroes yet, the new generation anti-hero heroes.

To conclude, such issues cannot have a plain black and white division, and the answers will always lie in the gray area. While media scrutiny may eventually tarnish every idol's reputation more or less, one cannot necessarily say that a society will not have any heroes, especially given the changing ideas of heroism.

7.19   Essay 19 (Own judgment vs. people's will)

> **Government officials should rely on their own judgment rather than unquestion-ingly carry out the will of the people they serve.**
>
> *Write a response in which you discuss the extent to which you agree or disagree with the recommendation and explain your reasoning for the position you take. In developing and supporting your position, describe specific circumstances in which adopting the recommendation would or would not be advantageous and explain how these examples shape your position.*

Understand the issue

We have to write an essay discussing whether we agree with the statement that instead of blindly executing the wishes of the topmost people, government officials should use their own judgment.

Discussion of the components of issue statement

Government officials – This issue restricts itself to government officials, possibly the mid-level ones who execute what the top levels in the hierarchy plan.

Should rely on their own judgment – The issue asks officials to use their own judgment. This suggests two things, one that officials are fully equipped to apply their own ideas to the plans that are passed down from higher levels, and two that the top levels share enough of their plans with the officials to enable the officials to use their own judgment about such plans.

Rather than unquestioningly carry out the will of the people they serve – This aspect implies that blindly following orders is not a good idea. This is an important suggestion. To simply carry out orders, especially seemingly negative ones, without full information officials should not execute. Officials should have the presence of mind to sometimes withhold implementation of work when plans seem incorrect. This should also be done when the will of those that the officials serve seems negative or not in the interest of the people. However, this should not be done randomly out of vested interests of the officials themselves.

Agree because	Disagree because
Government officials do need to assess the plans and not just blindly execute them	Government officials are not aware of the overall plan, and usually get only chunks of it to implement, thereby making them unable to assess those plans correctly
Sometimes, people in power plan selfish things not in the interest of the people, things which the officials can refuse to implement	Such behavior can cause blockages in the working of the bureaucracy and increase inefficiency in the system
	Officials can also do this to serve their own interests

The essay

There are as many ways to rule and manage, as there are people. Everyone has his own idea of what is right and wrong behavior, especially when it comes to government officials. The issue essay makes a good but slightly off recommendation that government officials should use their own judgment and not just blindly adhere to the wishes of their superiors. This recommendation has its merits and demerits.

On the one hand, it is true that many times big mistakes could have been prevented if people executing the wishes of the top people had exercised some caution before going ahead with the plans. For example, a man in Oregon was sentenced to actual prison because he harvested rainwater on his own property! Now apart from the discussion that is needed over the rules and policies that prevent rainwater harvesting instead of promoting it, those officials who prosecuted that man should have realized that the bad policies could have been offset by the executors of those rules who can apply them only if needed. Another terrible idea decided by the topmost people can be found in the state of Texas, where a computer repair technician is legally required to have a private investigator's license! There too, prudent and discreet government officials can prevent a lot of misery by recognizing the unfair demands made by the ones above them. Such officials have the choice not to harass law-abiding citizens over such trivialities and needless bureaucratic red-tapes. Thus, use of discretion on the part of the government officials can reduce or prevent incorrect, inappropriate or even needless decisions made by their superiors.

On the other hand, often times the freedom that government officials can exercise in implementing the rules can bring about grief to the people, delaying the processes and racking up inefficiencies already plaguing most bureaucracies. For example, when officials dig in their heels over petty rules and regulations, people are prevented from their legitimate pursuits. In many places, children are not allowed to sell homemade lemonade or cookies without getting permits! Also, allowing the government officials discretion can increase corruption and make vulnerable citizens further prone to harassment by officials, since officials could then use that discretion to further their own interests. Finally, often times, certain rules and regulations may seem trivial or unnecessary to government officials, who are not privy to the entire plan or the big picture.

Only the top people know the end goal and all the details, possibly on a need-to-know basis. In such a situation, if officials do not do their assigned parts, the whole plan can fall apart. For instance, tenancy laws require landlords to register tenants at the local police precinct, and obtain a permit. Any official who allows such permits to be issued without thoroughly crosschecking the details may inadvertently enable some fugitives or illegal. Thus, allowing such discretionary implementation abilities to government officials can backfire badly.

To conclude, there are both positives and negatives to the recommendation given in the issue. There is no clear winner as to whether officials should exercise their discretion. Distribution of power is always tricky. One has to delegate enough power to grease the channels of bureaucracy but not so much that any one entity becomes too powerful. This balance should be individually decided for each office by the supervisors and in turn kept in check by the public.

7.20   Essay 20 (Superiority of human mind)

> **The human mind will always be superior to machines because machines are only tools of human minds.**
>
> *Write a response in which you discuss the extent to which you agree or disagree with the statement and explain your reasoning for the position you take. In developing and supporting your position, you should consider ways in which the statement might or might not hold true and explain how these considerations shape your position.*

Understand the issue

We have to write an essay discussing whether we agree that machines will always be inferior to human minds, given that humans create machines.

Discussion of the components of issue statement

The human mind will always – The discussion of human mind, in comparison with machines, brings qualities like imagination, innovation, discretion, consciousness, adaptability, etc. in aspect. These qualities should be discussed with respect to machines.

Be superior to machines – The above mentioned qualities can be discussed to show how the humans can maintain their superiority over machines.

Because machines are only tools of human minds – The discussion of superiority of man over machine seems to imply that the two are at the same level and therefore comparable. However, machines are merely tools that humans have created to make their life better. Comparing man to machine is absurd, as absurd as comparing nature to human beings.

Agree because	Disagree because
Human minds have qualities that machines cannot have

E.g.: imagination, innovation, discretion | Latest technology shows machines that are strikingly similar to humans in certain qualities |
| Humans have the ability to adapt, and so far machines don't | Machines may get the ability to improvise, in the near future, creating the possibility of consciousness |
| Machines do not have consciousness in them that allows them to feel individual | This is a moot discussion, as one needn't decide the superiority. The use of machines is strictly to improve the quality of human life, and comparing man to machine is inappropriate |

The essay

The issue essay brings up a discussion that is lively and brewing all over the world, especially amongst technology fans. Since the advent of modern technology, it has always been debated whether there would come a time when the machines would be so smart and savvy that they would no longer remain merely tools of humans but becomes equals or rivals. In fact, many science fiction books and movies have been made using the premise of machines breaking free from their so-called human masters. Terminator series is the most famous example that springs to mind. Despite the phantasmagorical tonalities, the notion is possible, even though it is highly unlikely.

The side that believes that machines have the capability of eventually becoming superior to humans believes in the innovation abilities of the latest computers. These people posit that since artificial intelligence is becoming ever more sophisticated, there will come a time when such objects develop a consciousness. Once such individuality is chalked out, the objects would not be satisfied with their stations as only enablers of human beings. And being equipped with the best that technology has to offer, such objects would possibly establish themselves as separate entities, leaving humans without technology and possibly in danger. While the notion is scary and seemingly possible, it is quite unlikely.

The other side of the coin is the fact that humans are adapting creatures and have been able to survive, so far, quite a few threatening situations, anticipated or unexpected ones. One of the most important aspects to consider is that certain human qualities are intangible, qualities such as imagination, innovation, discretion, intuition, initiative. These qualities make us human, and enable us to battle fierce odds. The idea of creating human-like intelligence, or systems, is fascinating and scary, but regrettably, even humans don't know what it is to be human! Isaac Asimov famously quoted "the saddest aspect of life right is that science gathers knowledge faster than society gathers wisdom." Thus creating sentient objects right now seems unlikely. Even if such a situation arises, humans would be prepared for it. Despite the lack of awareness about the possible repercussions, the world survived the splitting of the atom, the making of the nuclear bomb.

Moreover, a notable idea to consider is that, this is an invalid discussion. Pitching humans against machines to judge superiority is not a fair or equitable comparison, given that humans created machines, and that humans and machines are vastly different entities. Such a comparison is illogical. In line with the issue, one might as well say that evolution and nature will always be superior to humans because humans were created by nature using evolution! The absurdity of such a comparison is thus revealed.

To conclude, while the idea of humans being compared to machines is intriguing, it is invalid. Also, there are concerns on both sides of the issue, concerns which can be addressed to ensure that the development of technology is smooth and hassle-free. Finally, the way the attempts of some groups trying to produce human clones were proscribed, as no clear ideas on possible repercussions existed, the same can be done for those projects that endeavor to manufacture sentience into technological objects should be suspended until clarity on its possibilities can be had.

Chapter 8

Speak to Us

Have a Question?

Please email your question to *info@manhattanreview.com*. We will be happy to answer. You questions can be related to approaches, analysis of arguments & issues, essay topics, or challenges in writing a 6.0 essay.

Do mention the page number when quoting from the book.

Best of luck!

Manhattan Admissions

**You are a unique candidate with unique experience.
We help you to sell your story to the admissions committee.**

Manhattan Admissions is an educational consulting firm that guides academic candidates through the complex process of applying to the world's top educational programs. We work with applicants from around the world to ensure that they represent their personal advantages and strength well and get our clients admitted to the world's best business schools, graduate programs and colleges.

We will guide you through the whole admissions process:

- ☑ **Personal Assessment and School Selection**
- ☑ **Definition of your Application Strategy**
- ☑ **Help in Structuring your Application Essays**
- ☑ **Unlimited Rounds of Improvement**
- ☑ **Letter of Recommendation Advice**
- ☑ **Interview Preparation and Mock Sessions**
- ☑ **Scholarship Consulting**

To schedule a free 30-minute consulting and candidacy evaluation session or read more about our services, please visit or call:

 www.manhattanadmissions.com **+1.212.334.2500**